DIGITAL REMAINS

*Thank you so
much for your
support!*

[signature]

DIGITAL

REMAINS

DEATH, DYING & REMEMBRANCE
IN THE TECH GENERATION

J.H. HARRINGTON

NEW DEGREE PRESS

COPYRIGHT © 2020 J.H. HARRINGTON

DIGITAL REMAINS

Death, dying & remembrance in the tech generation

ISBN   978-1-64137-937-3 *Paperback*

978-1-64137-738-6 *Kindle Ebook*

978-1-64137-739-3 *Ebook*

To my wife, JoHannah

Without you, I would not have found my voice.

CONTENTS

AUTHOR'S NOTE 9

INTRODUCTION 13

CHAPTER 1 DIGGING DEEPER THAN SIX FEET UNDER 27

CHAPTER 2 DEATH AND SOCIAL MEDIA 41

CHAPTER 3 FINDING THE WORDS 55

CHAPTER 4 DIGITAL REMAINS 65

WILL THE WORLD RUN OUT OF SPACE TO BURY THE DEAD? *81*

CHAPTER 5 THE PRINTED OBITUARY 91

CHAPTER 6 LEARNING FROM THE END 99

CHAPTER 7 MODERN NOTIFICATIONS 105

CHAPTER 8 THE REACH OF SOCIAL MEDIA 113

ASHES, WHAT ARE THEY REALLY? *121*

CHAPTER 9 FROM VISIBLE TO USABLE 133

CHAPTER 10 HOW WILL YOU SPEND ETERNITY? 147

CHAPTER 11 VIRTUAL FUNERALS 167

CHAPTER 12 HOW DID WE GET HERE? 173

THE PINE BOX PARADOX *185*

CHAPTER 13 DEATHITECTURE   195
CHAPTER 14 THE LEGACY OF A LIKENESS   199

THE SOCIAL MEDIA CLEAN-UP GUIDE   209
DIGITAL REMAINS PLANNING GUIDE   221

DIGITAL REMAINS PLAN FOR
PERSONAL RETENTION   225
DIGITAL REMAINS PLAN DESIGNATED
DIGTIAL REMAINS STEWARD COPY   233

ACKNOWLEDGMENTS   243
APPENDIX   247

AUTHOR'S NOTE

———

Dear Reader,

Thanatology—the study of death, dying, and bereavement—is a diverse field of study with the same intricacies and diversities of any other large field of study. While not widely available outside of elite universities, the subject is composed of elements of psychology, sociology, biology, archeology, anatomy, chemistry, business, political science, history, geology, religion, and many other fields of study. Thanatology teaches us as much about living as it does about death and dying, and it has been proven to increase the quality of life and happiness of those who study it by lowering death anxiety. Thanatologists work in various fields including the funeral industry, hospice, law, counseling, social work, education, and religion, as well as in medicine as oncologists, nurses, psychiatrists, and pathologists.

While this book touches on many aspects of death and grieving (specifically our digital presence, the evolution of death notifications, and some of the choices available to you and your family for funerals) I do regret that each of the many subjects of grief, mourning, and end of life do not receive the in-depth discussion they deserve in the pages of this book. With the restrictions of page numbers, I hope you forgive me for leaving a large number of these topics for future books. This book, for the most part, focuses on the digital aspect of death in the context of a rapidly progressing technological world.

Some may use this book as a means to plan ahead and utilize the Digital Remains Planning Guide. Others may use it after or during the loss of a loved one. Both are correct and encouraged.

This book brings complex subjects to light and hopefully ignites further examination and thought by you, the reader. We all have experienced or will experience loss in some way; my deepest hope is that, at the very least, you know you are not alone.

If you experience difficult moments reading this book due to memories of a loved one who has passed away surfacing, I'm okay with that. Having memories is healthy, as is giving them a moment of our time. Having these memories come to mind because you like or disagree with something I wrote is natural when reading a book on this subject. These memories can be painful, they can be joyful, and they can be many things all at once. I will never regret creating a moment, no matter how difficult it may be, for the memory of a loved one who has passed away. Instead, I am honored to be a part of your grief journey.

As an aside, I encourage you to make note of chapters I have titled *Urning the Answer*. These chapters answer some of the most common questions and gaps in knowledge I have heard or noticed. I hope they are helpful or at least give you powerful knowledge in a future conversation.

At the end of the book, you will find: 1) *The Social Media Clean-Up Guide*, a chapter that gives a site-by-site walk-through of how to transition or delete a social media account, and 2) *The Digital Remains Planning Guide*, a fillable guide that allows you to state your preferences for your digital remains and provide a copy for the person you assign to carry out these wishes, your Designated Digital Remains Steward.

If this book becomes overwhelming at any time, feel free to take a break or skip around. While the chapters were designed with a rough order in mind, the advice, knowledge, and stories within them will remain valid no matter the order of your choosing.

As a final note, know that there is no wrong way to grieve. But, if you are having difficulty with the death of a loved one that has prevented you from carrying out your daily life after six or more months have passed, I encourage you to talk to an expert. Psychologists and counselors can serve as beneficial resources, and if you are having trouble finding someone to talk to, your local funeral home or family doctor may be able to provide suggestions.

Another helpful resource to know of if you encounter someone in need is the National Suicide Prevention Hotline, a valuable resource that provides a toll-free 24/7 hotline available to anyone in crisis or emotional distress at 1-800-273-TALK (8255).

Go Forth and Live a Life of *Your* Choosing,

J.

INTRODUCTION

———

Chris was sitting in a small town in the heart of the Midwest, scrolling through the posts of his Facebook wall on a relatively quiet afternoon as he took a break from work. With the sun shining and the day going as most days do, Chris was content in the progress of the morning. The thought never crossed his mind that he would come across a post that would change the course of his day, the kind of news that sends a bolt of panic up your spine. Never would he have imagined this would be the way he learned one of the most critical female role models in his life, his grandmother, had died.

In a separate scenario, Ari from Los Angeles shared the funeral service information of a parent via social media. In a feuding family that had cut ties and communications to one another, a post on Facebook was the most logical way he knew to notify them, especially when no calls or texts were possible without having their phone numbers. A post on social media was the only resource that existed in his mind, even if it might ruffle the feathers of the few people who would not receive the notification in time for the services. The post succeeded in its intention: to reach people who were unreachable by any other form of communication in the time constraints that revolve around a traditional Jewish funeral service.

Chris, Ari, and others in their generation are among the first group to experience death, dying, and remembrance in this era of technology and wide-reaching online connections. The number of deaths we hear about can feel like an overload sometimes. We have all heard someone comment about how many celebrities have died in a short period while showing a tweet or post. Still, in actuality, we might just be hearing about deaths sooner and more frequently than before through the advances of social media.

Nearly three million deaths occur in the United States alone each year, according to the Center for Disease Control and Prevention.[1] If we pessimistically said that just two people post about each death on social media, we have more than doubled the amount we hear about people dying than we did with the single newspaper obituary format from the past.

We think of death, and the process that surrounds it, as unchanging—but it *does* change. In some ways, the experience can be amplified and improved with technology, or we can fight every step of the way, making it harder and more painful than it has to be.

The prevailing mindset is that funerals and death either do not change or *should not* change.

---

1   "Death and Mortality," National Center for Health Statistics, Center for Disease Control and Prevention, accessed on May 5, 2020.

"We'll do it like we always have before."

"Just put me in a pine box, I don't want to be any trouble."

"If it was good enough for them, it's good enough for me."

These sayings are commonplace when planning for final days and the days that follow. In a technological landscape that is changing faster than it ever has before, there may be new and more meaningful resources and options to aid in delivering a preferential remembrance. While your loved ones may still choose to tuck your physical remains beneath a marble headstone in a cemetery or inside a covered urn on a mantelpiece, other parts of you—your digital remains—could be left in view of anyone who knows how to use an online search engine that is accessible from just about anywhere.

If planned out correctly with new technologies, your physical remains and your digital remains can be linked by something as simple as a QR code, a barcode of sorts that can be scanned by a smartphone and redirect someone to a predetermined location on the internet. In an age of endless options and technical integrations for both services and remembrance, change might be what helps us all. From analyzing keywords in thousands of obituaries to new ways of understanding the grieving process, what we learn might change how you think about death.

I can say for a fact that biers, the wheeled stands that a casket sets on, make great race cars in empty oversized funeral home garages, a lesson worth getting caught over as a kid.

Family members were always around in the funeral home, whether it was Dad or Grandpa peeking out from the office or my great-grandparents and great-great-grandparents looking over us from creepy oil paintings on the wall, as we played all while funeral arrangements were usually being made in the next room over. **The divide between life and death was scarcely more than a veil in my childhood; a division in the relationship we have with death that is different for each of us.**

We have changed from a society that once picnicked and strolled through cemeteries like we do parks today to a society composed of many who wonder if they are being disrespectful if they walk through the headstones in the wrong way. We have highlighted through our actions the separations that have been created in society between ourselves and the subject and thought of death.

Death, when genuinely integrated instead of separated from life as you grow up, adds new colors and perspectives to the world around you. Granted, the physical presence of the dead was often behind a heavy velvet curtain over the past few hundred years or found in a restricted employee-only room more often than not, the idea of it is ever-present growing up in funeral homes. Seeing how some families benefited from one option and found comfort in it, while another family thought the same option might be the worst thing the world had ever witnessed, gave me perspective and created value in individual needs over cookie-cutter offerings.

I became fascinated by creating the ability for people to find funeral services and remembrance options right for them—regardless of cost or lack thereof—focusing more on a holistic approach to planning that balances wishes, budget, and meaning. As I would learn later in life, this has not been the case in many towns and cities across the country. So, I hope in some small way this book helps ease the divide and gives perspectives to those in and outside the funeral industry. In so doing dissolving distrust from the consumer purely because a comfort level does not exist on the subject, and letting funeral homes be a place they were originally meant to be. Places where services are designed for someone who needs help from any background helping develop and fulfill a holistic plan with full knowledge of potential costs that are involved in the option you are selecting. While it would be nice to walk into a funeral home with a hundred dollars and expect a private mausoleum tomorrow, that simply is not an achievable reality. If a client is equipped with the knowledge of what is out there and the cost involved in a realistic funeral instead of averages, we can potentially find common ground based in reality that brings the most good.

The funeral business is a service that exists to aid families with things that they want help with, after all. In that respect, the funeral industry is a service like any other, even boat-building, for example. While most might go out and buy a boat, built to the style and quality they want from builders that have focused their entire career perfecting boatbuilding to reflect what they have found to work best for the widest consumer base, others might have something different in mind. Some people might want to be more involved in the building process. Some may want to be involved in designing the hull or the selection of the sailcloth. Some may have a vision in mind that might be a simple rowboat while others hope to build a polished mahogany schooner but might need help from a master boat builder along the way. This kind of help is not unlike the help a funeral director offers to a grieving family. These individuals might go as far as going out to cut down and mill the trees, building the vessel by hand to satisfy their vision for the project to the level that satisfies the needs they have in their minds for what they need to do to connect with the project, thus finding meaning in the work.

Funerals in terms of involvement or options available are not much different. Some can find meaning in attending the service or fulfilling the image and traditions they have in their minds. For some, that includes involvement at every point while others find less comfort in that level of involvement. To others, the ceremony moves them the most, while others still look to what was done before as a standard to meet. The precious cargo, family and friends we are caring for when we seek out services like those involved with a funeral have come from our journey through life. Finding a balance in what helps our friends and family regarding the preparations and funeral of a loved one, preparations that we may not have the ability or want to do ourselves, is the reason funeral homes exist.

I grew up in a funeral home that focused less on the bottom line and more on what was right for each person. The aging building and funeral chairs from the seventies speak to that truth. The overflow seating chairs, older still, speak further to this longstanding business practice as they themselves reach a hundred years old. Seeing families select services ranging from a carnival in the parking lot of the funeral home to a quiet and somber evening for the sole surviving family member in an empty chapel provide insight. The knowledge of what's available and would best meet the needs of those involved play a key role in creating a space of mourning appropriate to the family being served. It's not only about receiving services but creating the path to remember and grieve in the most meaningful way possible. Personally, living by the adage: "What may be right for you might not be right for another person."

Throughout human history, human beings have evolved, and with us, the ways in which we choose to remember and mourn those who have died.

Ritualized burials have existed for nearly as long as societies, according to the archaeological record. Over that time, humans have practiced an array of diverse and meaningful traditions that center on death. Traditions regarding the preparation of remains have ranged from ritualized mummification in ancient Egypt to the practice of modern embalming. The integration and uses of fire in funerals have spanned from the funerary pyres on the banks of the Ganges in India to the near medicalization in comparison of cremations today. Practices of burial have differed from the temporary graves and crypts of Europe to the perpetual graves of the American cemetery. We mourn with ceremonies in public spaces, in our homes, and in designated facilities, with concentrations that range from eternal preservation to ecological, religious to secular, all while finding bits and pieces of these ceremonies to pass on and continue in successive generations.

For over 116 years, five successive generations of my family have played a role in gently laying to rest the remains of the dearly departed and have received the privilege of observing the evolution of preferences in differing communities. Among the standards, skills, practices, and philosophies each generation has passed down, on behalf of the generation that came before it, is the importance of being nimble and adaptable to change while respecting the needs of the individual.

With changes in technology and preference throughout human history, our communities have ebbed and flowed from conducting the services involved in a funeral, with some preferring to do everything personally. In contrast, others chose providers outside the home. Our local communities decided how services took place in a way that made sense, who might be involved, and where they are held. Still, with the digital archiving of lives through social media, nearly everyone with a connection to the internet has a recording of their lives, an archival practice that has not existed since the walls of a pharaoh's tomb.

As individuals, we have records of the highs, lows, internal thoughts, and feelings on a multitude of diverse topics that will continue to exist long after we are gone. We now have to think about how we would like those records of our lives, our digital remains, preserved or deleted.

Entering the longstanding funeral profession as a member of the tech generation, I confronted many new and old perspectives of what many often think of as a non-changing funeral industry.

Becoming licensed in multiple states across the nation, as both a funeral director and embalmer, and working and consulting for diverse firms that differed in numerous ways, the diversity of choices became more evident to me than ever. Working in settings from large to small, corporate to family-owned, new to old, multi-cultural to secularly focused, military to civilian, I developed a broad view of the ways the funeral industry connects to and does not connect to the communities they serve. I gained in-depth knowledge in the field of mortuary science before earning a post-completionary master's degree in thanatology, the study of death, dying, and bereavement. Then, utilizing my industry knowledge and education in economics, I was able to serve as the industry expert for the United States Government at the Department of Labor.

While true that many traditions carry on, continuing to search for new ways to help communities receive easily accessible care is vital. I believe that this process starts with knowledge. The *knowledge* of traditions. The *knowledge* of products available. The *knowledge* of what will be here tomorrow and what will be here for hundreds of years. Most importantly, the *knowledge* that you have a choice in how you want to be remembered and what is there for your loved ones when you no longer can be.

Many consider funerals widely unchanging and singularly focused on the act of the service or merchandise; I believe funerals always have been about remembrance at their core. But the ways we are choosing to remember are changing. With the integration of new options and resources in technology and social media, both small and large, when applied correctly they can change the funeral service for the better.

Over the past year, I set out to identify critical points in how new technology and social media have converged with funerals and the way we memorialize and remember those who have passed. This new technology can provide valuable resources and options that allow for more meaning, personalization, and opportunities to connect than any generation has had access to prior.

These new choices enable us to enhance memorialization through personalization. We must take a look at how technology is marching ahead and creating a path in death, funerals, and the remembrance of others and where we might look for *the obituary section of our time* once newspapers, as we think of them today, become a thing of the past.

If you're like me, you want to know what your options are as well as things you might have overlooked and open the closed doors that divide us from services available at funeral homes, crematories, and more across the world. This new viewpoint grants us reassurance in the ways we choose to transition into a place of remembrance.

With knowledge comes the comfort to ask questions. You have the ability to *pull back the curtain* on the mysteries of the funeral and all that surrounds it. This new knowledge lets you pragmatically plan for the options and services you want before you need them.

While talking about death is never easy, hearing some of the following useful and, at times, odd stories and ideas might prove to be extremely useful to you, such as:

- You will learn how to gather insights about how to utilize social media as a tool to notify circles and remember loved ones.
- New and exciting alternatives to traditional burial or cremation provide insights about the future of death-care that few know about before they are needed.
- As a reader, you will attain new knowledge on the grieving process.
- You will even learn whether your ashes are beneficial to your garden.
- You can rest assured you are neither the first nor last to wonder if picking that plain pine box gets you what you want, and you will examine the underlying aspects that you may be looking for in a funeral to get a full picture.

But why stop there? You can discover if you need to consider the rights to your hologram, as well as identifying other choices that *no* generation has had to make before.

So, join me. Let's discover some of the myriad options that exist on the topic of funerals. Let's look at what social media and death have to do with each other and how they can be integrated to benefit those we know. Let's learn a bit about something that few think about but all of us will have to experience. Let's pull back the heavy velvet curtains of the funeral industry and discover as much as we can about what we perhaps have not thought about or did not know was accessible to those who plan ahead.

At the end of it all, this life is what we make it... and the path we choose in remembrance.

"We all die.

The goal isn't to live forever,

the goal is to

create something that will."

—CHUCK PALAHNIUK

CHAPTER ONE

DIGGING DEEPER THAN SIX FEET UNDER

———

At social events, friends and family sometimes introduce me as a "party favor" of sorts, not just because I'm a good storyteller but because of the types of stories new acquaintances invariably ask me to tell. The conversation inevitably starts something like this:

"What business are you in?" or *"So what do you do?"*

The person who asks these questions usually asks them with an expectation of a bland response in hopes of common ground. When you are in my line of work, however, you can expect two things when answering this question: either a prolonged silence or a look of a surprise. And then, people usually say:

"Oh, really? How fascinating! I have a question for you."

The types of questions that follow typically fall into one of three categories.

Category #1: Macabre (myths/rumors/morbid curiosities)

I get the feeling these questions have been lying in the back of the person's mind but were perceived as too morbid to utter aloud. That is, until they hear the words, "I'm a funeral director."

"Is it ever creepy working alone at night?"

"What is the strangest thing that you have seen?"

"Have you ever had to dig someone back up?" (You mean exhume a body, I think to myself.)

"Do they ever sit up?" (Anyone who tells you this happens is lying to you. I am sad to disappoint.)

Category #2: Personal Experience

These are more follow-up statements that use my, "I'm a funeral director," to launch into a personal experience with death. This category diverges quickly between those who actually need to talk to someone or verbalize their grief and those who are taking the rare conversational opportunity. Those sharing personal grief, I am absolutely willing to talk with, no matter the setting. If this is the place and time that feels right for the person sharing, I'm more than willing to offer a listening ear. The other path usually consists of lots of 'I' statements that take on an oddly bragging tone with experiences around death. I'm not a big fan of the latter but acknowledge it too as a mode of communicating a grief experience and as something that deserves a polite and listening ear.

Category #3: Pop Culture

We have all seen a movie or TV show that shows, even for a moment, how we interact with death. From Jack Black in the movie *Bernie* to scenes from *NCIS* (insert city here), any number of questions can come out of the woodwork. Sometimes these questions are about the accuracy of how things are portrayed. Questions like:

"Would that really happen if..."

"Do you personally play all the songs on the organ?"

"Have you seen that show Six Feet Under? Is it really like that? "

By far, the HBO series *Six Feet Under* is the most referenced and asked about. The show aired five seasons between 2001 and 2005 and depicted a family who runs a funeral home and their complicated lives that still exist in the meantime.

"So, have you seen Six Feet Under?"

"Yes."

"Is it really like that?" they ask.

"*Sure, but the drama from one episode is roughly equivalent to the drama experienced throughout an entire career.*"

Venturing too far from this simple and admittedly vague answer creates awkward situations more often than not. Usually, the person asking either realizes they were seeking answers outside *their* comfort zone or shifts the conversation to a personal past loss when they were *not* prepared to take a deep dive into their grief journey at the moment they asked. Either way, many factors such as setting, affect, tone, and passion are all indicators you have to look for in a person before you answer this question.

My full answer to the question, "So have you seen *Six Feet Under?*" however, is far more interesting, in my opinion, and requires a little background.

Anyone who has watched *Six Feet Under* can recall the iconic introductory main title sequence. The roughly one-and-a-half-minute show open is composed of one ethereal scene after another, punctuated with staccatos of orchestral strings and chimes written by Thomas Newman, who won an Emmy for his work. The main title sequence takes the viewer along the path of a body on its journey from the gurney to the grave in short clips, as designed by Danny Yount. Yount even won the Primetime Emmy Award for Outstanding Main Title Design in 2002.

One of the title sequence's iconic scenes features a table lined with framed pictures, depicting an older woman. To make this scene, the production and direction crew used what was available and found some family photos of Yount's still-living grandmother at the time. Several years later, those same photos were used and displayed as a part of Yount's grandmother's actual funeral, which was held in the very same family funeral home where I lived and worked at various points in my life. *Six Feet Under*'s logo depicts the stark, black and white artwork featuring a tree, with roots spread just wide enough and just deep enough to accommodate a casket—but in its place lies the show's title. A printout of this logo signed by Danny Yount, which he was kind enough to offer in passing before his own grandmother's funeral, still sits in one of the arrangement offices, placed discreetly between an urn and informational pamphlets.

What viewers often missed in the show, however, is the life knowledge and realistic confrontation with death and mortality that the main title scene broaches with the audience. In a talk, courtesy of the Australian Broadcasting Corporation, Danny Yount, the director and designer, spoke on his thoughts on the themes behind the scene.

"So for *Six Feet Under*, [...] I really liked the singularity of the imagery of the foot and the gurney. Those are the two things that kind of set me off on this, and I liked that you couldn't see the person," Yount said, referring to the person on the gurney in the opening scene that maintains anonymity through the sequence of scenes only being caught in glimpses.

Then Yount dove into something that went a bit deeper, discussing how the topic of death and mortality developed in the design of the scene.

"I was a little bit concerned about the death metaphor in that whole theme, you know, that the show deals with, and I didn't want it to be something negative. This gave me a chance to really test my abilities as a communication thinker, how do I turn this into something that is more ethereal and surreal and something that's more that has a lot of depth to it," Yount shared.

The reality of death being more than a singular topic that instantly brings up a personal memory of loss in a person's mind was in Yount's mind after beginning his work on this scene. The idea of death is a complex weave of emotions and thought that carry large amounts of weight in our minds. "Life and death are very serious matters, especially what our approaches to it are and what we believe about it. So, I kind of went down that road. They liked it. Obviously."[2]

Yount then went a little deeper and addressed the process and initial designs he had to go through by showing much more detailed scene sketches. These initial sketches went more in-depth into the life and imagery associated with a mortician's life and the confrontations that exist with death. They showed more graphic moments and focused more on the individual who was the funeral director and what was being done than the anonymous figure escorting the deceased body on its journey to the grave.

"I had made some [thumb]nails to kind of try to test my idea. I wanted [the scenes] to be centered around the life of

---

2   FORA.tv, "Designing the 'Six Feet Under' Title Sequence - Danny Yount," January 15, 2010, video, 4:42.

a mortician. Sort of a daily working process. I think I was a little more literal about it than I should have been [in the initial designs]. But you know, you kind of have to go there first," he said.[3] Yount quickly realized that his mind needed to play through and process the extremes of the idea and images of death before he was able to then look at the subject in a new way.

"And I think as a younger designer, I used to be afraid that if I did something that was clichéd or literal just straight out that it would ultimately become the end product. Whereas now I kind of look at it like, sometimes you have to start there, you know. Sometimes blue is blue and red is red and you just kind of start there and then as my process develops then you really question yourself and you really kind of sort these things out as you go along. And that's how I like to work anyways."[4]

By confronting the images and ideas around death and the life of a mortician in his mind first, Yount was able to refine the image he had created and begin to process his thoughts on the image of death. He realized after his first attempt that he would not have been able to reach his final product without taking it farther and letting his mind process what it needed to do first before beginning to understand the ideas that surrounded the subject. This process is similar to our need to first relate the topic of death to a personal loss we have experienced before we are able to think about the how's

3   FORA.tv, "Designing the 'Six Feet Under' Title Sequence - Danny Yount," January 15, 2010, video, 4:42.
4   FORA.tv, "Designing the 'Six Feet Under' Title Sequence - Danny Yount," January 15, 2010, video, 4:42.

and why's that surround the ideas of death and dying as a topic.

The avoidance of death and subject matter that surrounds it, like funeral imagery, encompasses an idea in psychology referred to as Terror Management Theory.

According to the Terror Management Theory, all human behavior is motivated by the fear of one's own demise, giving rise to a state of anxiety that arises when we confront the awareness of our own mortality (mortality salience) with the desire to survive.[4] The anxiety produced when mortality salience is activated is reduced via mechanisms for thought control, such as proximal and distal defenses.[5]

Proximal defenses are initiated when Mortality Salience is activated, i.e., when thoughts about death enter our consciousness. They are rational and allow us to escape such thoughts by fixing our attention on other things, reducing the attention focused on oneself, or trivializing one's own vulnerability to death. [6]

When we begin to process ideas that may incite thoughts into our mortality, we begin to prepare ourselves to think about topics that address mortality. These topics can include planning our funeral, writing the outlines of our obituary, buying a burial plot, and finding meaning in the remembrance ceremonies that we choose.

---

5   Gordillo, Fernando. "The Effect of Mortality Salience and Type of Life on Personality Evaluation," *Europe's journal of psychology*, 13(2), 286–299.

6   Gordillo, Fernando. "The Effect of Mortality Salience and Type of Life on Personality Evaluation," *Europe's journal of psychology*, 13(2), 286–299.

What I find to be the essential first step is beginning the dialogue. Decisions that take place around death, funerals, and our wish to be remembered are not rip-off-the-bandage situation topics. Taking care of things quick and fast does not always deliver the desired results, only a result. And that's something *Six Feet Under*'s producers get right. Each episode starts with a death. Mortality Salience is activated and apparent as the characters confront difficult discussions. Those discussions, often depicted between the episode's grieving family and the funeral director, are not unlike the types of discussions I have had with grieving families over the years. In moments of chaos and calm, helping the grieving family was the priority.

The often-dramatized background of the family behind the family funeral home in the show did touch on the reality of dynamics and balance between work and life a funeral director has to have in the real world.

As a kid, going to the grocery store or leaving large community events like a play or church was the longest, most excruciating part of my life. It was at these times that people would stop a funeral director (my dad) and talk. These are not just everyday conversations about the weather; more often than not, they are immediate deep dives into personal grief. These are the moments that go unacknowledged, the moments of active listening, and being there for the people who had lost someone in the past, with little to no personal benefit, just the knowledge that these moments are part of the job if you care about what you do. No work/life separation or time off exists when it comes to a grieving family.

These moments are not on the clock. The funeral director learns this counseling through the school of hard knocks most of the time, but these moments do exist. It does not matter that they were running out last minute to get something for a dinner that was almost ready; if someone needed to talk in the cereal aisle for thirty minutes, dinner could wait. The oven was used to keep meals warm at times like these and not a word was mentioned about the delay when dinner was finally ready. The time given with a listening ear was always far more important. If the kids were promised ice cream after the show and someone started easing into a conversation at the door, ice cream could wait for another time. If you were standing at a funeral in a foot of snow on a windy hill and you were notified that your family home was burning down, calmly finishing the burial and helping the family back to their cars was the only thing that mattered at that moment. All these events happened countless times to me as a child or while working a funeral as a funeral director myself.

A priority shift occurs for people who genuinely take on the responsibility of working in the funeral industry for the right reasons. This shift at some points is visible as an external calm in the face of urgency, which is captured in *Six Feet Under* every once in a while if you look for it.

The grieving family is going through one of the hardest days they might go through in their lives psychologically while at a funeral. Within the grieving family alone, panic, fogginess, false urgency, shock, and any number of other unpredictable factors and emotions may arise, as well as sudden temporary upsurges of grief or STUGs.

STUG: A Sudden Temporary Upsurge in Grief is a moment that is triggered by a visual cue, scent, sound—really any environmental or internal trigger that causes an intense emotional response. Often in association with the memory of a loss. A "STUG" is an intense and unexpected wave of grief that arises in a person. Even though sudden overwhelming emotions can be very upsetting, STUGs are common and healthy for the bereaved. They can be very intense and can interfere with the ability to think or talk clearly, or the ability to temporarily continue with regular activity.

STUG's tend to happen more frequently immediately following a death before becoming far less frequent as time passes. Having a random upsurge in grief many times after a loss is common, and it can be triggered by something as simple as a familiar smell. This intense emotional response seemingly comes from nowhere and can cause panic and concern for the individual and those close to them, before leaving just as quickly as it onset, and justly so. After all, the emotion seemingly comes from nowhere. The simple knowledge of a term for what is happening can provide some level of reassurance and normality to a concerning event. Knowing the term, STUG, can help some to begin to realize and remember a simple lesson: there is no right or wrong way to grieve!

On that note, if you or someone you know has debilitating grief that greatly interrupts daily life for an extended period, often many months after a loss, it may be a sign of complicated grief. Talking to or seeking the advice of a trained psychologist or counselor can be very helpful. If you are unsure of how or who to talk to in a case like this, your local funeral home should be able to provide a suggestion or referral to a professional in this area.

The funeral director is responsible for helping guide the family, and often the other people attending the funeral, along the path they have chosen for a funeral. These are the most real moments, the helping moments, that stand out to me in the show *Six Feet Under*, ignoring the mistakes or inaccuracies most people assume I am looking for in the show.

Sure, every other funeral director, morgue attendant, doctor, and I also look for any procedural inaccuracies or if a body looks dead on the embalming table, but those details are easier to spot and disregarded almost as quickly. And while not everything may be similar to how such a job is portrayed on television, the core idea and exposure to death that is all too real and often not talked about is presented in between the dramatic episodes that keep viewers engaged and coming back for five straight seasons to HBO.

Not only is the idea of how we choose to be remembered important, but the way we create outlets to do so for the people we leave behind. Creating an atmosphere to mourn is something worth looking at and then looking at again. We need to allow our minds to find some logic and understanding in the nearly incomprehensible subject matter that is addressing our mortality and planning our path of remembrance or that of our loved ones.

Some of the most memorable ways we memorialize those who have passed away are the creative and close to home plans we develop. For some, a creative and meaningful solution for remembrance might be the placement of a treasured photograph or a memorial plaque added to a bench in a nearby park. For others, a final resting place for a loved one's ashes might very well be under a tree in the garden just outside their window.

CHAPTER TWO

DEATH AND
SOCIAL MEDIA

———

IS A POST JUST A POST?

He let it ring a few times, the call that would soon change everything.

Chris felt like they had just left the house when he got the call. It could not have been more than half an hour, an hour at most, that he and a close friend had been out doing some shopping and running errands around town when he felt the buzz of his phone in his pocket and the ringtone sounding. You know the one, the ring of an old-fashioned telephone.

The house had been eerily silent in the days following his family's departure. Going to work every day was his only reprieve from the overwhelming reminder of all that he was missing out on. Going to work, of course, was also the reason he was missing out on all of it. Having to stay back from a family vacation to the Grand Canyon had been kind of a bummer, to say the least. In the days that followed his family's departure for vacation, Chris had lingered around the house and gone to work. Work had kept him in town after all, but the empty house was more of a reminder of missing out on family time than was bearable. The yearly family trips had always been one of the highlights of his year. All of the cousins, his aunt, uncle, mom, and grandma all loved the chance to be together, and the vacations were a secondary but fun side effect of the main objective: togetherness.

Missing what sounded like a fantastic experience, hiking down into the Grand Canyon itself was even more disappointing for Chris, but he knew he'd be able to join on next year's trip. If he had to ask for the time off a year in advance, that was fine with him. Missing another family trip was not going to happen, and after being alone for half a week, that was final.

His phone ringing had admittedly brought both delight in seeing that it was his mother calling to share some trip highlights, as well as a sting at the thought of missing out. He was excited to hear what the day's adventures had held. Knowing it also would make him feel more distant than ever, Chris answered.

"Chris, I'm going to need you to sit down or pull over."

Those are words that never come before anything good, Chris remembered thinking.

What followed was an explanation that can never truly be prepared for until you are in the moment. Catching most of what was said, only distracted by reactionary thoughts of panic that were eased by instant logical calmness, Chris absorbed that his grandmother had collapsed on their walk through the canyon.

In short, the paramedics were on their way, and a promise of a call with an update once they got to the hospital and knew more was offered. There was little he could do but wait for news, being a thousand miles away, so he spent a moment processing what he had just heard. And then, he and his shopping companion, a lifelong friend, headed home.

The drive home was quiet, a combination of not knowing what to say and willing the phone to ring with good news. By the time they reached the front door, the anticipation of the impending call was already wreaking havoc on Chris's nerves, and the search for a distraction became paramount. Sitting down on the couch and turning on the television helped but only for a moment before his mind wandered back to memories of his grandma.

A commercial jingle on the television triggered a fond memory of his days in the high school band. It was hard to think of a single performance that did not involve her getting the best seat.

She was always excited while pretending to be calm, ready to see two of her favorite things in the world working as one: her grandson and music. It had to be pure love and enjoyment for her, considering he played the tuba. Thinking about it all only made quick flashes of worst-case scenarios cross his mind all the more. Chris needed a distraction, and fast!

"I decided I should take my mind off things and scroll through Facebook to pass the time," Chris recalled during our conversation.

Chris's habit is a frequent reaction most of us have today. Whether a lull in the conversation, a moment of rest while we wait, or a way to shut off for a few minutes, logging onto social media and scrolling is cathartic. It provides a welcomed release and distraction. The endless wall of videos, photos, and memes was just the distraction Chris wanted.

Barely five minutes after he'd begun mindlessly moving through his Facebook feed, Chris stopped his scroll on a post from his cousin. No vacation photos. Just these five words.

Well, my grandma just died.

"I remember seeing that post," Chris said, "and I immediately threw my cell phone across the room at the front door and just curled up into a ball on the couch and started bawling my eyes out. I laid there for a good fifteen minutes, just crying."

A nightmare scenario had become a reality, hidden in the posts of friends and family, like a snake from the weeds. The words from a simple post struck Chris's mind without context or warning, triggering intense emotions and pain in an instant. It was a few hours after reading the post before Chris finally heard the old-fashioned ring tone again.

His aunt's picture appeared on the screen of his smartphone, and answering took a second longer than usual because he knew what she was calling to tell him. Opening the door to news you do not want to hear is a hard thing to do.

"She attempted to break the news to me," Chris remembered. It had been several hours since his grandmother had passed away. "I remember telling her, 'Yeah, I already saw it on Facebook.'"

"Who would have shared such a thing like that?" his aunt asked, shocked.

"I told her that my cousin had posted it, and she apologized profusely and felt terrible that I had to find out the way that I did."

"The damage was already done."

Death notifications on social media, while reaching the widest audience possible at the press of a button, also present new challenges and standards of etiquette that can aid or diminish our psychological health and mental well-being. The fast and evolving technologies that allow us to communicate the world over bring with them new challenges for the rare and sensitive occurrences that happen in our lives. The challenge remains how best to distribute the information in a time and way that does the least harm while also informing others.

Chris finished by saying, "I heard of her passing in one of the worst ways… I definitely think it would have been quite different if I had heard it another way… I am able to currently look back at it and tell the story in a joking manner, but it took me quite a while before I was able to think of that moment and seeing that post without becoming full of anger and sadness."

It can be a shocking and surreal experience to find out someone so crucial in your life has died, and the way you hear about such an event can play a significant factor in how you remember that experience.

Chris, like many others, brought his story forward with a simple request for experiences with death and death notifications and social media posted on Facebook. Like many other responses similar to Chris's experience, I reached out to hear his full story, with many of the stories sharing close parallels. While unfortunately, I could not dedicate an entire book to sharing these experiences, Chris's experience with death notification and social media shared many of the details that I was able to hear about that all rooted poetically in response to a request on a Facebook post.

Similarly, I shared the same post requesting experiences that people had with social media and death or death notifications on other social media websites. Just like on Facebook, Instagram delivered similar messages. While many of the responses were similar to Chris's experience of coming across a post by surprise, several others expressed different perspectives and circumstances. Several stories presented themselves as remarkably similar in family dynamics, and overall outcome to each other. In the interest of confidentiality, I selected the name Ari to share the genuine intricacies, experiences, and quotes gathered from interviews with several individuals, all springing from my post requesting experiences on Instagram.

Ari is a Los Angeles funeral director. The story he shared with me, while similar to Chris's in some ways, diverges at other key points.

"My father died in a hospital near his house," Ari shared. "He had prostate cancer and had been on hospice for less than twelve hours. I was handling nearly everything that had to do with the funeral preparations, except for the registering of the death certificate and burial permit."

Being the person who is taking the lead when making arrangements for a parent or family member can be a challenging and draining task that requires lots of planning, phone calls, and decisions. It can be even harder in a family that has all but cut ties from one another. Even with the knowledge that Ari had acquired working in a funeral home himself, some of the challenges still seemed to be overwhelming when it came to notifying friends, family, and coworkers.

With time in short supply, as Ari's father was Jewish and required traditional aspects in his funeral, two days seemed like an impossible time frame to notify people he had no means of contacting. He had no phone numbers, no email addresses, not even real addresses, nothing. When he went back to his father's house to pick out clothing to take to the funeral home, his aunt was sitting in the dining room at the computer. She had logged onto his dad's Facebook account, attempting, with some difficulty, to write a post about the service information. In her mind, a post stood the best chance of reaching as many of the family members he still had connections to as possible, as well as some of his friends and coworkers.

Having experience writing countless obituaries, Ari sat down with his aunt and, within a few minutes, had a useful post that included all the service information someone would need including times and locations. It was the same information Ari would send to the funeral home to put on their website later. The obituary was up. There, on his dad's Facebook wall, friends and family would be able to access all the information the family had in the most convenient way Ari could imagine.

The funeral services came, and except for his mother, who had been divorced and estranged for some time, testing the limits of familial relationships that were already rocky with sharp and pointed comments, the services went well. The production crew that his dad had worked for had even seen the post and canceled productions of the television show they produced for the day of the funeral, leading to more than three hundred of his dad's coworkers attending the services. For Ari, it was a significant and meaningful tribute seeing so many people take time to be there.

A few days after the funeral, Ari got a call from his grandmother on his mom's side, who lived in Palo Alto a few hours away. She was devastated. Having just heard the news of the death, she was distraught, and she could not understand why she had been left out. Even though her daughter had divorced Ari's dad many years before, they had still maintained contact and shared updates on life with one another. How could no one have cared to share the news of his passing with her? She would have never seen a post on Facebook, not having an account. She could not believe it. She was hurt. Emails presented enough of a challenge to a woman who felt much more comfortable with a tangible paper medium than anything on a computer. It had been Ari's mom's job to inform her side of the family outside of the Facebook post, and for one reason or another, she had not passed along the news to her mother about her ex-husband's funeral.

Ari felt terrible.

Emotionally charged experiences like those that surround death and complicated family dynamics are not easily solved overnight, as is the case with Ari, who is still navigating the struggles and rifts from the loss of his father.

The opposite side of a post, the one from the view of the person posting, can also carry logic and reason too. While a post that notifies the intended audience can be a shock to the reader, at times, it may be the only option.

With the nearly endless possibilities that exist with technology and social media, there do exist gaps, which can prove challenging when social circles like those available on Facebook do not overlap with the full extent of our social circles in the real world.

Challenges of how we present the information posted on social media are not the only aspect to consider when sharing information like a death notification. The way the audience on social media perceives some posts can carry a great deal of weight as well.

College students historically fall within an average age bracket of eighteen to twenty-one years old.[7] Thus, in the year 2020, they were all born between the years 1999 and 2002, and in 2010 were around ten years old. Now take into account that the iPhone first hit the market in 2007 and that Facebook launched on February 4, 2004.[8] [9] Facebook started accepting non-college email addresses to register in September 2005, and everyone with an active email address in September 2006, with a minimum age to become a user set at thirteen years old.[10] The average age someone first gets a smartphone is about ten years old, according to a study by Influence Central in 2016, down from twelve years old in 2012.

Considering the information, this group of college-age adults is the first group to have no perspective of the world without access to an iPhone or Facebook, allowing them to have a view that differs from other groups on how social media might be both properly and improperly utilized, perhaps more than any group that came before them.

In a discussion that came about as another response to a post asking for experiences with death, death notifications, and social media on Instagram, a group of college women replied and considered the new dynamics that social media brings to death through a group interview as they took a break from

---

7   Brett Molina, "When is the right age to buy your child a smartphone?" *USA Today,* August 27, 2017.

8   Sarah Phillips, "A brief history of Facebook," *The Guardian,* July 25, 2007.

9   History.com Editors, "Facebook Launches," A&E Television Networks, October 24, 2019.

10 Ben Gilbert, "It's been over 12 years since the iPhone debuted — look how primitive the first one seems today," Business Insider, July 22 2019.

studying for winter finals. The conversation centered around the conversion points of death and social media. This group found the subject immediately relatable, in that they recently had heard of two members of their high school who had committed suicide within the span of the last few months. Watching everything unfold from a distance via social media presented them with several interesting aspects of how social media presented new challenges.

"While it [social media] brings good things to the table, such as being a way to grieve as a community and informing people who might not have known otherwise, it also has some downsides," one offered.

The core concepts of social media become challenging and even present downsides when used in the same way we write posts about our daily lives.

"Since social media is pretty self-centric," another said. "It almost feels sometimes like people who weren't even necessarily that close with the person who passed spin it into something tragic that happened to themselves."

There is something to be said about the traditional way of receiving the notification of a death and service times in the obituary section of a newspaper. They also acknowledged that coming across anything close to home as they would be ruffling through the pages of a newspaper was a rare event in their lives. Physical newspapers were not a common form of media for anyone in their group of friends as far as they knew, even though newspapers were free and readily available across campus.

"There is something kind of beautiful about handling these situations with care and grace, and I think that social media [the way it exists today] sort of takes that away or taints that," another shared.

Facebook and other similar social media indeed have the proper connections that you would want to notify for a funeral. The group also acknowledged that even though they would want all of their friends on Facebook notified, they doubted that their parents would even think about logging onto their accounts. They also agreed that none of their parents, as far as they knew, would have a means of accessing their accounts even if they did think about it.

This random sample of college students discussed possible advice and solutions for how death notifications and their presence on social media might be handled in an ideal world, with a goal that as many people as possible that a given person knew, or that would care to see the news, would be informed. They came to a conclusion that satisfied their current view of the online etiquette they would want to see on social media.

Summer, a twenty-year-old sophomore, summarized the lesson: "We feel like the best solution is just to post the obituary, and then whoever wants to can share it so that the words come more from what the family wants to share and how they want to share it. It honestly might not be very possible, though, with the nature of social media because people are always going to elaborate and say what they want."

Is a post just a post? Maybe yes, maybe no, but the information that is received is genuine. We can find joy, sorrow, excitement, anger, and sadness all in the posts we come across as we scroll through our feeds. Being mindful of this might be the key to successfully relaying sensitive information like the information shared in an obituary.

The depths of social networking via sites like Facebook, Instagram, Twitter, and others are a continually evolving conversational dynamic in an even more changing world. We as a community are still finetuning how we encounter and spread delicate information in a way that is the most beneficial to the audience that will receive it. Pausing and thinking of the people that will view a post and how this audience will receive the information are central in the effective and beneficial sharing of information on social media. While finding the right words when discussing the loss of a close friend or loved one is not often easy, understanding how these words, and the meaning behind them, are received plays a vital role in the success of a post.

CHAPTER THREE

FINDING THE WORDS

———

What do you say when someone you know has experienced the loss of a loved one? Do you share a quick memory that came to mind about the deceased with their family at a visitation?

Is it okay to just say, "I'm sorry for your loss?" Is that the wrong thing to say? Is it worse to say nothing at all? What do you say when you're told someone, whether close to you or not, has died? How are you expected to respond?

These are all common thoughts and worries people have when approaching someone who has experienced a loss. Expressing condolences is a form of interaction many of us have little experience with, but sometimes the simplest sentiments mean the most.

Offering meaningful support to someone who is grieving is a challenging hurdle that we all have to encounter in our lives. Whether in the form of a tear emoji on a Facebook post, a brief reply to a shared post, a text sent to a friend showing support, or words offered in person at a funeral, these conversations take most of us out of our comfort zones. They make us aware of topics we avoid thinking about.

Different generations have differing comfort levels with different modes of communication. Some generations prefer phone calls instead of text or a quick face-to-face over an email; the information and sentiment are the significant part over all mediums in regards to condolence. The meaning of the comforting words can be what makes the connection even more meaningful and frequently has the most impact on a person grieving in the long-term.

In-person notifications are an age-old and easily overlooked practice in today's world of technology. A simple "Happy Birthday!" on Facebook after being reminded by the website of someone's birthday is different than mailing the person a card in the mail or showing up at their desk with a cupcake, each carrying different weight. These interactions become almost more real in person. While the intention might be the same, the message carries different weight in each example. In some relationships, a simple message is more appropriate via social media and carries, a "someone is thinking about you" sentiment while others are more appropriate in person.

If your spouse chose to write *Happy Anniversary* on your Facebook wall, leaving it at that without some real-world interaction, most might see it as missing the mark. Celebratory events seem to even carry some additional leeway in comparison to more serious events in terms of communications online and in person. At times, in-person communication can be the most meaningful mode of communication, while simultaneously being one of the most challenging for both the person delivering and the person receiving the information. This is especially true in a world that is transitioning more and more to virtual communication habits.

We often hear many similar responses from those around us when they discover that we have lost someone close to us. These responses are rooted in a mix of the proper sentiment and a loss for what to say. In these events, many of us defer to words heard many times before in a similar scenario. These are often accepted for what they are, words of condolence, and are exactly what you should say if they feel appropriate to you.

The person receiving these words of condolence, however, may not be ready to hear these words for what they are, meaningful heartfelt condolences. Instead, some in the throes of grief might hear a simple, "I'm sorry for your loss" in an entirely different way than it was meant to be received. In these instances, what is said and what is meant can be lost in translation.

"I'm sorry for your loss."

"I'm sorry."

"She is in a better place."

"Heaven gained an Angel."

"He was a good man."

"They were a beautiful soul."

These are all common expressions heard at funerals that fill the place of words that are hard to find. These are very appropriate condolences and more often than not are very appreciated. It can be painful to think of a particular memory of the deceased that could be shared with the person grieving, but in some cases, through that pain can come loving sentiment or helpful words from personal experiences.

If you want to share a quick memory of a time that sticks out in your mind about the deceased, mentioning it to someone at the funeral is a perfect time to do so, if not later in passing. This helps solidify that their loved one is remembered or left an impression on the world around them. Be it emotionally or with a smile, kind words are very appropriate to share. Not every condolence has to be tear-filled.

Sometimes, in rare circumstances, however, simple condolences can be heard in the wrong way. We are not always ready to listen to the words that those around us are offering. As a funeral director, I have had several people ask how to respond to statements that seemed irrational to them at the time of a visitation or wake, explaining that while what they heard is commonplace, they suddenly felt confronted by the words meaning something different at that time in their grief. They feel guilty for hearing words they know are meant in a heartfelt way, which instead they interpreted cynically on the receiving end of the condolences.

Grief can be a disorienting experience for some. I have listened to people share what they heard, and then offered what they felt like saying in reply but refrained. It was clear to these people at the moment that their feelings were somewhat misplaced, but the way they heard common sayings stung nonetheless. They knew the words offered were from a place meant to help. They later felt bad they even had certain thoughts as our discussion continued, and acknowledged many of these thoughts were coming from a place of internal anger with the death or being overwhelmed in the moment.

The following are examples of internal commentary that followed someone sharing a common condolence that they then shared with me in one particular discussion following a visitation. These were the thoughts and inner dialogue that occurred in the person's mind as they heard time and time again the same words of condolence throughout a funeral and visitation.

The condolence that was offered was: "I'm sorry for your loss."

This internal dialogue struck the person receiving the condolence: Mom's not lost. I know where she is. She dead. She is lying right there in the casket.

"Heaven gained a good one/Heaven gained another Angel."

Well, Mom didn't believe in any of that, and neither do I frankly, but I'm glad you think so.

"How are you going to manage without her?"

I have been the one caring for her 24/7 for the last few years, but I suppose being a housewife myself means I'm useless to you.

"She's in a better place."

I thought here with me was a pretty good place, but I guess you don't think so.

These examples are not meant as sayings to stay away from, but instead, to give you the reader context that words can carry differing meanings at different times in our lives, especially during times of grief and bereavement. Each of them can be heard in a number of ways to the person receiving them, and if you are offering them as a heartfelt sentiment, these words are landing in the right place, even if it may not feel perfect at the time they are shared.

After some time had passed, however, these words of condolence became a comfort and were acknowledged as such by the person sharing with me. It took this person time and an ability to process what had happened to be in a place where they could hear and accept the sentiments expressed by friends and family, which is perfectly fine. There is no wrong way to grieve. This person acknowledged that words were falling on them in a different way and became aware of it. Grief can manifest in many different ways, mentally and physically. Becoming aware that something is different is healthy because something *is* different. You are becoming aware of a world that the person you lost is now playing a different role in.

Neither the expressions of common condolence nor the tone of these words was at fault and neither was the way this person received them. It was a matter of willingness to hear what was said that stood in this particular person's way in the end. Some of us may never truly be ready to listen to condolences or be at a place where we can offer heartfelt sentiments to a person when they are needed. Still, the act of presence and a willingness to provide kind memories, via post or spoken word, does carry weight when they might be needed most.

Condolences are often appreciated in act alone, but sometimes they have the potential to mean the world to someone in the moment when received at the right time and place. I came across a post about a friend who had recently been part of a podcast interview about his experience with loss and grief. A story that, while I had known bits and pieces from accounts over the years, was new to me. In his brief post on Instagram sharing with friends, he was able to sum up an individual experience with someone offering condolences that had significant meaning to him.

"The day my Mother died, many folks said: 'I'm sorry!' But the words of support I remember most came from a college friend who had lost his parents a couple of years earlier: 'I hope you can find a new normal, sooner than you think possible.' His words came from painful experiences—different from my own—but with a common thread of understanding. I hope by sharing my experiences with loss... I can be of help to folks going through a grieving process."

He added, "I find strength in knowing I am not an orphan let adrift at sea, but rather I am surrounded by others who have sailed similar waters and can offer perspectives on how to chart my course through grief's murky expanse. I know I benefited from such generosity."[11]

11 Benjamin Gunning, "Words of Support." Instagram, January 21, 2020, Accessed January 22, 2020.

In some cases, hearing words that are shared in a meaningful way with the knowledge of a similar prior experience can elevate the sentiment offered, making the statement all the more pertinent. This experience of past loss allowed a friend to reach within to find words learned in the school of life. Similar to the reason some people find comfort attending group sessions with others who have experienced similar losses to their own. A message of hope, learned through past experience, can be extremely meaningful at the time and place a person is willing to hear words of hope and comfort. Through forcing ourselves to confront a loss and the experiences we have had in our own lives, it becomes possible to share words of condolence and hope that are ready to be heard all the while accepting that *no two losses are the same.*

Each of us can learn so much from our past experiences. We can reflect on what we needed in a tough time in the past and use that to help others. While it can be uncomfortable to be a presence in someone's grief, a simple, quiet moment such as shared eye contact or a squeeze of the hand can mean the world to someone when words are hard to find. Many common sayings are very appropriate in most settings, but speaking from the heart when expressing helpful words can carry meaning. What seems to come through most often is an honest sentiment from a place of significance, regardless of the words expressed.

So, what do you say when you're told someone has suffered a loss? Maybe you do not say anything at all, and that's okay. Maybe you offer a memory that came to mind that included all of you. That's great too. Maybe a simple pat on the shoulder feels right in the moment. Gauging the moment can offer more than words sometimes ever could. Every interaction is unique, and every sentiment is heard in time. Know that these words and your presence are appreciated.

If you are unable to find the words, know that any condolences you are sharing will be heard, and the fact that you are sharing a sentiment means the world!

CHAPTER FOUR

DIGITAL REMAINS

———

It can be difficult to visualize all the material that composes our digital remains, and it can be even more daunting to control its reach.

What happens to your online presence when you die?

How long will the information that you have put online throughout your life exist?

Who will see or have access to this information after you die?

When we begin to take a slightly deeper look at what will happen with our online information in the future, it becomes apparent that it needs to be addressed. Let's dive into some essential advice and ideas that will help you traverse the now growing task of managing what will become of your digital remains.

To refresh, information that exists of us online—the pictures, posts, blogs, articles, and mentions—composes our digital remains.

Digital remains are the temporary and perpetual imprints, both direct and indirect, of our lives and existence that are present in digital forms on the internet, in the cloud, or coded into other extractable sources. We exist for all intent and purpose digitally living on in a way as coded 1's and 0's that make up our information online, as well as physically. Ignoring the eternal uses of what exists of us online, our digital remains, would be a grave mistake!

The idea of our digital eternity exists widely in pop culture references that range from the Nine Inch Nails song, "Zero Sum," which contemplates our lives as 1's and 0's, to movies like *The Matrix* that go a little farther and dive into the fictionalized idea in which everything, including the world we live in, is at its base a computer program composed of 1's and 0's. If we step back and look at the real-world applications of our digital remains, however, it becomes clear that they are not an abstract idea but rather something we realistically have to address in the modern world.

> *Digital Remains: the temporary and perpetual imprints, both direct and indirect, of our lives and existence that are present in digital forms on the internet, in the cloud, or coded into other extractable sources.*

The integration of your digital remains into your will can highlight the preferences you have for your online information to a Designated Digital Remains Steward, who is someone you specify to carry out your wishes for your online presence. Incorporating these wishes into your end-of-life planning might be one of the most efficient and official ways to express the preferences you have for your data online once you are gone. These additions might include the passing on of access to your cloud storage, passwords to multiple sites, and access to the content that exists in your inboxes. These wishes could also express the preferred path you have chosen to those you leave behind that should be taken in regulating the public exposure of your image, likeness, and information on social media sites.

We will go into some of the details of how and what to think about when considering each of the larger social media sites later in this book, as well as in *The Social Media Clean-Up Guide* at the end of this book.

MONETIZING DIGITAL MUMMIES

Carl Ohman and Luciano Floridi from the University of Oxford, Oxford Internet Institute, suggest that people's digital remains, like our social media activity and online history, should be regarded in the same fashion as the human body and treated with care and respect rather than manipulated for commercial gain.[12]

Ohman and Floridi's paper points out new repercussions of technology that involve our digital remains that have, before today, not been in the spectrum of possibilities, stating: "Firms such as Eterni.me and Replica now offer consumers online chatbots, based on one's digital footprint, which continue to live on after users die, enabling the bereaved to 'stay in touch' with the deceased."

---

12 Ohman, Carl & Floridi, Luciano. An ethical framework for the digital afterlife industry. Nature Human Behaviour. 2018.

Future monetization could also potentially come in the form of targeted ads in the future based on life events of past generations. One extreme example of this might be if your parents divorced as you moved off to college and then you happened to divorce around the same time in your life; your children might receive ads for divorce attorneys right alongside ads for dorm room supplies for their children regardless of the health of their marriage. It might also be the case that images of you from throughout your life could be drawn from to create a holographic representation of you after you are gone. If this hologram were to be combined with predictive conversational technology and the voice recordings from your life we mentioned, the idea that your grandchildren could make some additional money on the side by leasing the rights to your hologram to any number of companies for advertisement is possible.

Some people might say, "If you can do it, go for it. I'll be dead, who cares." I, however, am not sure I want to be the holographic face of male enhancements one hundred years after I'm gone. The very thought of this kind of *Digital Zombification* sends a small shudder down my still-intact spine.

While these are extreme scenarios that very likely will be focused on at length in the future, they do highlight the possibilities of metadata and the need for control and regulation or planning in the area. This control can begin with the designation of what you would like done with your digital remains and who you would like to be in charge of them.

You may have told your children or been told yourself, "Everything you put on social media or online is 'forever.'"

Few people consider that forever includes a time beyond their death when they no longer are the ones who can feel the repercussions of what exists online. For this reason, selecting someone who will be in charge of carrying out your wishes regarding how you want to exist on the internet after you pass away is essential. Making your preference clear regarding whether you would like to have everything on your social media accounts deleted or leaving your memory preserved as tangible remnants and heirlooms from your life helps make this decision easier for those you leave behind.

The alternative is selecting that your online presence becomes a resource that is accessible from anywhere that may be needed. Will your grandchildren benefit more from an online memorial page where others can share their memories and pictures from your life, like your Facebook wall or a memorial page on another form of social media? Will your spouse benefit more from a tangible remnant or place that brings with it a meaningful connection?

Whichever option you choose, or if you possibly select an option somewhere in between, consider who might find the most meaning in how you wish to be remembered, keeping in mind you are picking the path that is best for you and those you leave behind.

We could start by looking at Facebook, which in most user scenarios has or will have the most substantial chunks of an individual's life archived and organized in an easy-to-navigate manner. The immediate decision someone has to make is if they want their digital remains, the digital remnants of their life on the internet, maintained in perpetuity or not. If not, the settings options do allow for the ability to have your account deleted indefinitely, once Facebook is made aware of your death. The deletion selection does mean that someone would have to reach out to Facebook via the memorialization section of the settings menu and provide proof of a connection to you with confirmation of your demise. We will go into details about this process and what information is needed later.

Communicating these changes to Facebook is a small and efficient step that only relies on someone in your friends or extended family to reach out to direct family members who can then contact the company, as is preferred by the company, to have the page removed. A potential downside does exist; this page may have been helping someone process their loss. The deletion of the Facebook profile, while in the wishes of the deceased, may be a surprise to the person who finds comfort viewing it.

If you choose to have your profile converted to a memorial page, Facebook has made it very easy to assign a legacy contact to take charge of converting and maintaining the memorial page of the person who has died. This option is in the memorialization section of the settings.

The third option that is selected by omission and currently has the highest usage due to the memorialization option becoming available sometime after the initial launch of the social network means doing nothing and letting your profile exist as it does presently, basically choosing not to plan for a time you are not around to manage your Facebook profile. By not doing anything to your account after you die, your page is essentially frozen in time, only altered by comments on your past posts until the company eventually discovers it and either converts it to a memorial page or deletes it. While being a page that is not converted to a memorial page or removed due to someone notifying the company is an option, it does stand to reason that many of these accounts will be converted to memorial pages by friends who notice them and send a request to the company.

The benefits of assigning a person to convert your digital remains on Facebook to a memorial page (a legacy contact) in many cases prove to be a very valuable mode of memorialization. Your memorial page is designed to provide a shared place of remembrance for those who wish to find comfort in the memories and pictures. This conglomeration of posts documents life in greater first-person detail and organization than was often available in the past. This form of technological remembrance is available at a moment's notice, anywhere the site is accessible. If someone chose to search your name while walking through the cemetery, they could potentially find your memorialization page on Facebook or another website as one of the first results. This search functionality would enable them to access a small portion of the story of your life, among the several other search results that might only offer mix-matched snapshots of your life and leave out large sections of your digital remains.

MEMORIALIZED ACCOUNTS ON FACEBOOK
Two official options exist for your Facebook page after you pass away.

You can assign a legacy contact that takes charge of your memorial page, converting your existing page to a memorial page at the necessary time, OR you can have your page deleted upon notification of your passing to Facebook. If you choose not to select that your account be deleted at your passing, your page will be converted to a memorial page when Facebook becomes aware of your passing. According to Facebook, "Memorialized accounts are a place for friends and family to gather and share memories after a person has passed away."

As part of your memorialized page, the word 'Remembering' is added next to your name.[13] If you allow others to post on your wall currently (depending on your privacy settings), others will be able to post memories for others to see on your timeline. The photos and posts that you shared in the past remain visible to those you shared them with, meaning that if you would like more or fewer people to see your past posts, your privacy setting may need to be adjusted to achieve the audience distribution that you desire.

While your memorial page is a resource to those who may find a connection and meaning in using it, your profile will no longer appear in birthday reminders, ads, or as a suggestion of friends you may know. Any pages for which you serve as the singular administrator on Facebook will also be deleted once your page is converted. So, if you would like a page that you singularly administer like a high school class alumni page or running group to continue, for instance, you should add at least one additional administrator to the page.

---

13 "Memorialized Accounts" Help Center, Facebook, last accessed May 28, 2020.

Pages and groups are also a great resource that are available to memorialize someone with the ability to share with a selected audience. An added benefit of memorializing your page is that your account is secure from anyone else attempting to log into your account. Even after death, Facebook maintains strict privacy policy and reminds users to "keep in mind that we can't provide login information for someone else's account even under these circumstances."

Finally, **no one** can log in to a memorial account once it has been converted. Meaning that if you have not chosen to have your account deleted nor selected a legacy contact that can manage your memorial page, your memorial page cannot be altered.

What exactly is a "legacy contact?" Much like assigning someone to be in charge of your life once you are no longer able to make decisions, such as is the case with a durable medical power of attorney (DPOA), which allows you to select someone to make medical decisions for you when you cannot. The legacy contact option allows someone you trust to maintain your memorial page after you are gone. This person can be selected from your existing friends on the site and designated in the memorialization section of your Facebook settings. If you would like to change this person at one point or another, you also have this ability if demographics or dynamics change in your life.

The value of this contact can be very beneficial according to Facebook: "The legacy contact can control who can post tributes on the memorialized account and who can see those tributes." Your legacy contact will be able to share a pinned post, which allows them to share a final message that you may have written before your death—enabling you to share your last word and final goodbye. This message will remain at the top of your memorialization profile until it is changed or removed as well as have the ability to share service times or other pertinent information. This person can change your profile and cover image if perhaps you would like a final picture from a point in your life that is more recent or from a happy time in the past to serve as your memorial image.

If you would like everything that you have shared on Facebook to be put in a downloadable copy, Facebook has allowed for this in your settings, and your legacy contact can acquire this. The ability to save someone's posts can be a valuable resource to some who may choose to have a savable or physical file of these posts that can be downloaded, printed, and saved with other tangible items they have left archiving their life.

Additionally, having a copy or file of these shared posts is helpful if you would like to have your legacy contact delete your account after some time, which they can do. The legacy contact cannot log in to your account and can only maintain the page once it has been converted to a memorialized page. They also cannot add or remove friends that you had or read any of the messages you sent before your death.

BEYOND FACEBOOK

For advice on how to delete or convert other social media accounts including Instagram, TikTok, YouTube, Pinterest, and many others, refer to *The Social Media Clean-Up Guide* at the end of this book.

WHEN A HEADSTONE TELLS A LIFE STORY

Another company that is using the ease of technology to tell a story of remembrance while creating a community is Keeper. After getting a Keeper account and completing a short family tree to establish connections to your nuclear family (parents and grandparents), you can create your obituary told from your perspective or a telling of life events, creating all of this long before you die.

This site works with a similar principle as other sites in that you designate an individual to convert your Keeper account into a live page of remembrance after you pass away. You can also create an account on Keeper for a loved one who has passed away.

Mandy Benoualid, co-founder and CEO of mykeeper.com realized when looking at niches in a mausoleum at her grandfather's funeral that there may be a need for a connection point between what we see at the cemetery and online resources that enabled a stronger connection to the deceased person's life. This connection could allow us to find a way to discover the enriching stories that were behind each of the lives lived in a cemetery.

"It happened really at my grandfather's funeral at an indoor columbarium," Mandy shared in our conversation. "It was an indoor place, and there were glass niches. Niches are essentially these glass cases where urns are placed behind glass. And people can put keepsakes and pictures, you know they are typical things that the family can leave. I came across one of these niches that had a blank CD, with *Dad's Work* written on it. It struck me as weird. My dad is a techie, and we're standing there wondering what could be on a blank CD like that. We were curious. Nothing came up when I googled his name, but it must have been important to his family and to that person, and their legacy. They obviously wanted to find a way to preserve it, to showcase it, in a way, his work. There are so many stories and dashes between their entire life story, and so the thought was, you know, what if you could learn about all of these people in the cemetery? That's what we went with at founding. Our thought was really to make it [Keeper] like a social media kind of platform, really following similar principles. The goal is really for interactivity in that way, so that's really how it started."

An added functionality that allows more ease and convenience is the ability to attach a small QR code to your headstone in the cemetery that directs the person who scans the QR code directly to the memorial page you have created on the site. Oxford dictionary defines a QR Code as, "A machine-readable code consisting of an array of black and white squares, typically used for storing URLs or other information for reading by the camera on a smartphone."[14] They are markers that can be read by the camera on your smartphone that direct you to a designated website. Some smartphones have this technology included as standard software, while others require you to download a QR code reading app.

Mandy shared in our phone interview, "It's the fastest way to get somewhere when you're on your phone, so people could just simply pick up their phones and scan it, and they

---

14   Lexico. s.v. "QR code (n.)." Accessed May 28, 2020.

get brought to the page where you would learn about that, and the QR code markers come in different colors including metal [to match the stone or personality]. There is one on my grandfather's grave."

The way that we see the shift happening in society in how people receive information that someone in their lifelong social network has died is changing with the integration of technology. The change from notifications via newspapers is diminishing, while new platforms are becoming available online.

Keeper, along with other sites, is being integrated into funeral home technology and notification systems filling the void when it comes down to how people in a community acquire their information about a death or funeral. With new abilities to subscribe and receive email updates and new place to go to see information via online resources, these new websites are beginning to play a critical role in death notifications.

"One of our clients in New Mexico is not super remote," Mandy continued. "But they don't have much of a newspaper or any[newspapers] in the section of their state." At one point in the past, there was only one real place to look for an obituary, and people in a community depended on a newspaper. "Now it's switched to digital and to the point where even the local radio station [in this client's area] goes to one of our clients' websites to look at the Keeper pages and the obituaries and use it to talk about the recent deaths. So, in some areas, it is kind of taking the place of newspapers as a place to go for obituaries."

Doing work in advance on sites like Keeper allows someone who utilizes it as a source of memorialization the ability to design and present stories and post in a way they want. Exercises like writing your obituary or life story ahead of time can be beneficial in creating headspace that is typically strayed away from in life. It allows us to look back and find the events that happened in life that we see as essential and consider how we want others to see this information. It helps begin the conversation in our minds about what might be beneficial to those we leave behind.

Today, we no longer find limited options but myriad choices regarding our memorialization after we are gone. With large chunks of our lives documented online through various social media accounts and tokens of achievements from our past, we now have to choose in what way we utilized these resources after our active presence is converted to a memorial presence online.

With the ability to create a memorialization platform as part of your planning process that is linkable to other social media accounts and platforms, the key is convenience and accessibility. With an easy path to find and convenient meshing of linked accounts, it becomes easier for a community of those around you to form and find out they too hold a piece of the past, that when shared, brings everyone closer together.

DELETE IT, DELETE IT ALL... OR DON'T.

If you choose to have as much online information as possible deleted, resources now make this possible. Companies now exist that provide the service of removing as many past traces of your online presence from the internet as possible, including your social media accounts, websites you hosted, blogs you contributed to, and much more. A key factor to consider is what you have online and who is using these memories. Be it for comfort or a way to grieve and remember, our digital remains are as real as our physical remains, and providing those we leave behind a connection point can prove to be a valuable resource.

The complete deletion of your online presence can have cultural implications, however. By completely deleting your online presence, you are leaving the memory of your time on Earth solely in the physical world and the minds of those you leave behind. If the idea of final death is important to you, you might very well expedite your Final Death by choosing to delete as much of your digital remains as possible, which is something to think twice about before choosing that path.

WHEN ARE WE TRULY GONE?

For some, death occurs at the point when someone stops breathing; for others, it is when the heart stops beating, cardiac cessation. Brain death is even divided into various categories that range from partial to whole-brain death. Certain definitions of death occur far after the funeral. Cellular death is complete when cellular activity ceases in the body. Further still is the death that occurs when our tissue and bone structure have completely decomposed and are indistinguishable from their surroundings.

Then comes an idea found in the Disney Pixar animated movie *Coco* released in 2017 that brings forward the concept of "Final Death" through the telling of Miguel and his family's generational ban on music and his extraordinary journey to discover his family history. The concept of Final Death becomes the focus and struggle that underlies the plot of the film. Final Death occurs at the moment at which you are no longer remembered, the final time you are thought of or mentioned by the living.

Does leaving an online presence of our digital remains online delay our Final Death? Does completely deleting our digital remains expedite our Final Death, or derail all memory of your existence?

Our digital remains are a genuine part of our existence in our current technological world. How we choose to continue forward with our online presence is a decision for each of us individually. Each plan is unique to our comfort levels and wishes. Just as an Advanced Care Directive helps those who are left in charge of our decisions when we are unable to decide for ourselves. Allowing individuals to designate everything from "do not resuscitate" requests to what to do if we end up in various stages of a coma. So, too, do we need to establish our wishes for the future of our digital remains, if only to help those we leave behind to carry out these decisions and be confident in knowing what we prefer.

WILL THE WORLD RUN OUT OF SPACE TO BURY THE DEAD?

———

Cemeteries are everywhere.

They are scattered across country and cityscapes from one town to the next all around the world. Will the finite amount of real estate we have on Earth be filled with caskets and monuments as the world grows ever more populated?

We go to the cemetery for many reasons: to bury our dead, to mourn, to grieve, to spend time remembering those who were lost. These visits serve many essential purposes for the human condition, but how much space are we giving up for that opportunity? Do cemeteries take up that much space? Will we eventually run out of space to bury people? These are all common thoughts expressed when someone makes decisions because of perceived scarcity, which in this case is assumed to be land.

Let's start by breaking down the question, and we will discover just how much land it would take to bury everyone on earth with a look at some of the economics around death—or "Deathonomics"—and break this question down by the numbers.

According to the population clock at census.gov, the world population currently stands at roughly 7,594,275,500 people as of August 2019 and growing.[15]

To calculate the amount of space needed to bury everyone in the world, we need to establish the required area for one single-depth burial plot. While more space-efficient options do exist, this is an excellent place to start. Let's assume that each person's burial plot would adhere to the current traditional Western burial standards for this scenario. With this assumption, we can determine that each person would need a plot of land with a surface area 2.5 feet wide and 8 feet long, or 20 square feet.

Twenty square feet is enough room for the casket inside of a burial vault to be buried below ground level. The two-and-a-half-foot width leaves enough room on each side of the casket or burial vault for the next burial to occur without disturbing the prior grave. The eight-foot length also leaves additional room back at ground level near the head end of the casket for a headstone. (Monuments, grave markers, tombstones, or gravestones are most commonly located at the same end of the burial plot as the deceased's head, thus headstone.)

---

15 "U.S. and World Population Clock," U.S. Population, United Stated Census, Accessed May 29, 2020.

So, to calculate the land area needed, we multiply the current world population (7,594,275,500 people) by the standard size of the burial plot (20 square feet), which totals 151,885,510,000 square feet of land.

That is a lot of square feet!

Now, since so many square feet are hard to visualize, we can convert the square feet needed to square miles required. If we divid e our total (151,885,510,000 square feet) by 27,878,400 square feet (the number of square feet in a square mile), we come to just over 5,448 square miles required.

You might say at this point, "That seems like A LOT of land area!"

So, let's look at land areas roughly equivalent to the required land area of 5,448 square miles that we would need to bury everyone currently on Earth. Thanks to census.gov, we can also find the total area for each state as well as separate figures for land area and water area.[16]

Since burying people under bodies of water is markedly more difficult, land area totals are the focal point. Besides, we should leave those lakes and waterways as pretty scenery in our unified planetary cemetery.

Let's start with New Jersey, which has a total land area of 7,354 miles squared. That's right; we could bury the entire

---

16 "State Area Measurements and Internal Point Coordinates," References File, United States Census, Accessed May 29, 2020.

world on roughly three-quarters of New Jersey and still leave the turnpike to get around and room for that beautiful shoreline—a small area of land compared to the size of the world.

Alternatively, we could look at Connecticut, which has a total land area of 4,842 square miles, plus Rhode Island, which has a total land area of 1,034 square miles. Combined, they form a total area of 5,876 square miles of land. United these two states would provide a beautiful and scenic waterfront cemetery with 428 square miles of land to spare.

At this point, logic sets in, and you might be thinking that maybe we should go for less prime real estate. Perhaps we should find somewhere more rural and economically responsible.

I offer the six northwest counties of Kansas in the combined rolling pastures of Cheyenne, Rawlins, Decatur, Sherman, Thomas, and Sheridan Counties with a total land area of 6,009.55 square miles.[17] That leaves 561.55 square miles to spare for fountains, parking lots, an airport for visitors, and nearly all current buildings to stay in place!

So, next time you are flying over the Great Plains at 35,000 feet, you might think to yourself, "NO, we are not running out of room to bury people, and this could hypothetically count as visiting my relatives." A question we might consider however is:

---

17 "Land Area and Population Density in Kansas, by County," Institute for Policy and Social Research, University of Kansas, Accessed May 29, 2020.

How can we simultaneously use this land for the good of ourselves, society, future generations, and the future of our planet?

As technology grows, so too does our ability to explore cemeteries today from the comfort of our home. With innovations in genealogical websites, our history and the location of our ancestors are easier to find than ever. Other helpful sites designed to share the stories and histories of those buried like findagrave.com utilize cemeteries as a gateway to our own family stories that allow us to see someone's grave without having to navigate the countryside.

Naturally, the next question that pops into most people's mind**s is:**

"What if everyone were cremated?"

Human ashes (cremains) do take up far less space than a casket after all.

Having served as an industry expert and economist, it is safe to say I am fascinated by the numbers behind determining the space needed—a kind of Deathomonics analysis of the question, if you will. In the event you are not a numbers person, however, I feel I should warn you, determining the space needed for cremated remains has slightly more math involved than determining the space needed for burials. But do not worry, you will get a football reference and talk of diamonds for sticking it out.

Using the same population figures from above, we again start with a current world population of 7,594,275,500 people.

Next, we would need to assume the average volume of each person's cremains. The average standard adult urn is 200 cubic inches (in³) according to CANA, The Cremation Association of North America.[18] We should also recognize that it would be best if we found a final space that is slightly too large, instead of too small, to fit the entire world's ashes in a mega-ossuary. (An Ossuary is a location that holds multiple human remains.) So, we will assume that each person will take up all 200 cubic inches of an urn.

I think it is safe to say we would not want any overflow, so we will try to find a space slightly larger than we would actually need.

If we decide that the average person will take 200 cubic inches of space for their cremains each with an average weight of five pounds, we first need to multiply 200 cubic inches by the current world populations (7,594,275,500 people) to get 1,518,855,100,000 cubic inches. Next, we will convert our volume in cubic inches to cubic feet. One cubic foot (ft³) equals 1,728 cubic inches, so by dividing our total cubic inches by the cubic inches in a cubic foot (1,518,855,100,000 in³ / 1,728 in³) we get 878,967,071.759 cubic feet, which is the volume in cubic feet needed for the world population's ashes.

---

18 "Industry Statistical Information," Cremation Association of North America, Accessed May 29, 2020.

Since not all of us can visualize that many cubic feet in our minds, let's determine the volume in cubic feet of something we can easily picture.

The size of a regulation Olympic swimming pool according to FINA, the International Swimming Federation is fifty meters long by twenty-five meters deep with a minimum depth of two meters.[19] To determine the cubic feet of the pool, let's convert meters to feet. (1 meter = 3.28 feet) meaning the dimensions of the Olympic swimming pool are now 164.04 feet long, 82.02 feet wide and 6.56 feet deep. To find how many cubic feet are in the Olympic swimming pool, we multiply the length by wide by height (164.04 feet x 82.02 feet x 6.56 feet) to get 88,261.92 cubic feet.

Now we simply divide the volume we need for the world population's cremated remains (878,967,071.759 cubic feet) by the cubic feet in a regulation Olympic swimming pool (88,261.92 cubic feet) to discover that we would need 9,958.62 Olympic swimming pools to store the world population's cremains, assuming the weight of the cremains in one large mass would not compress under its own weight.

That many swimming pools are still hard to conceive of, so let's look at something much bigger.

Many estimate that the Dallas Cowboys Stadium, home to the famous Dallas Cowboys football team located in Arlington, Texas has a volume of 104 million cubic feet.[20]

---

19 "FINA Facilities Rules," Swimming Pools, International Swimming Federation (FINA), Accessed April 28, 2020.
20 "AT&T Stadium," Twitter, Posted January 27, 2017.

If we divide our total volume needed for everyone in the world's cremains (878,967,071.759 cubic feet) with the size of the Dallas Cowboys stadium, we discover that *8.45 Cowboys Stadiums* would be required to hold the current world population's cremated remains with the total weight of the ashes alone being 37,971,377,500 pounds or 17,220,579.4 metric tons.—which is slightly more than the weight of 195 US Navy Nimitz Class Aircraft Carriers.[21]

Since there do not happen to be nine identical Dallas Cowboys stadiums, where might we be able to place all of the cremains in one place that already exists?

I'm so glad you asked. The *Mir Diamond Mine* in Mirny, Sakha Republic, in the Siberian region of eastern Russia, is one of the largest manmade holes in the world and has an estimated volume of 198,000,000 cubic meters or 6,991,380,000 cubic feet, meaning it could hold *7.95 times* the amount of ashes of the current world population (6,991,380,000 cubic feet divided by 878,967,071.759 cubic feet).[22] Talk about having room to spare.

While spending Memorial Day in Siberia at a mega-ossuary with the world's cremains or at a unified world cemetery in northwest Kansas might be a tough sell to the family, we can rest assured that the space exists if needed and is the furthest thing from scarce.

---

21 "Facts File," AIRCRAFT CARRIERS - CVN, United Stated Navy, Accessed May 29, 2020.

22 Rhett Allain, "How Much Dirt from This Diamond Mine?" Wired, January 22, 2013.

"*Death is not the opposite of life,*

but a part of it. "

—HARUKI MURAKAMI

CHAPTER FIVE

THE PRINTED OBITUARY

Muhammad Ali — Janis Joplin — Edward Lowe

What did these people have in common? They were all featured in *The New York Time*'s Editorial Obituaries.

The *New York Times* print edition's obituary section is the place one would go to find individuals who have lived lives worthy of a featured obituary presented to the broadest audience of daily readers. Once you consider the high (and I do mean substantial) cost of a paid obituary in most papers, you will realize that even having a paid *NYT* printed obituary in today's world implies a certain level of success. The prominence of the editorial feature seems to take on even more significant weight.

The editorial obituaries section that generally takes up half of the six-column page falls under a different set of standards than the normal paid obituary section. Instead of being written to adhere to a stringent format by a funeral director or family member, editorial obituaries are written and researched by professional journalists. Recently, the *NYT* has even begun issuing obituaries from key figures in the past who were not featured at the time of their death for a number of political and social issues at the time, thus allowing female and minority features to be recognized for the true world changers they were.

The editorial obituaries in the *New York Times* have seemingly one qualifier for entry as Bill McDonald, their obituaries editor, revealed in a question and answer forum.

> *"The basic questions we ask are: Is this death national news? Did this person have such an impact on this world that his or her death is something our readers should be told about?"*
>
> —BILL MCDONALD

In most scenarios, editorial obituaries are written in advance to accurately portray the life of a person who made an impact on the world without the strain of a deadline. Considering many of the feature obituaries are for names that are not recognizable in most households, this is important forethought. Take, for instance, a past editorial obituary headline: *Edward Lowe, whose accidental discovery of a product he called Kitty Litter, which made cats a more welcome household companion and created a half-billion-dollar industry, died at a hospital in Sarasota, Fla.*[23]

While this is a person who undoubtedly changed many lives and left a product that will endure long after his passing, the

---

23   "Talk to the Newsroom: Obituaries Editor Bill McDonald," The New York Times, September 25, 2006.

information of a life lived outside of the national limelight does take a bit more time to track down.

Not everyone who has left a tremendous impact on the world in the many diverse fields that exist has a household name, after all. Writers often need to dive deep into research and interviews to find the full story.

The need for accuracy and immediate editorial response has led the writers in this office to compile a backlog of individuals who have an obituary written for them in advance. Each is selected for a variety of factors, including age, health, and aversion to risk. Once the need for the prewritten obituary arises, minor review and updating is added, making the process as efficient and error-free as possible.

For the writers, this does not come with a sense of decreased importance for the advanced work. As it turns out, the act of writing obituaries in advance for others carries the knowledge of the importance of the work. When asked if the obituary being the last word carries a burden, Bill McDonald said, "Many people think of a *Times* obit as the last, last word. So it's a double weight."

The journalists who write these obituaries take it upon themselves to create a life story that includes the highs and lows of a given life. "But our beat is," Bill continues, "like sports, dining, opera, or nuclear physics, part of the human story. (The last chapter, I suppose.) Good obit writers have to possess something of the historian in them."

THE SHIFT FROM PRINT TO DIGITAL

The shift of the paper to online editions has created a new obstacle for people who have become accustomed to reading the obituaries in a physical paper as part of their typical daily foray. This routine can have deep meaning if you look at it in the right way, as we will learn with Lux's story in the next chapter.

While some sections of the paper now get large tabs as part of the digital version of the paper, tags reserved understandably for their daily headline at the top of the news cycle, other sections are less highlighted. Sections like the obituaries are often delegated to a sub-tab that has to be navigated to or sought out with some effort. The relegation of the obituaries to a sub-tab is not the end of the world for most of us, but it does signal a shift that has more implications to our lives than at first sight.

This placement of the obituaries section in a sub-tab on most online papers has opened up an opportunity for third-party applications and websites to pick up the slack and publish the obituaries of the common person outside the newspaper. This move takes away from the convenience of a one-stop-shop with the newspaper but allows for easier access in other ways—namely affordability.

In nearly all obituaries in the past, the funeral directors working with the family were the ones who wrote the obituaries, with family members writing those the funeral directors did not. Now local funeral homes can offer online obituaries on their websites at little to no cost, eliminating the need for an expensive published obituary in a paid obituary section. Thus, the common person has less of a barrier to summarize a life in four lines and more ability to receive a full obituary than ever before. From local funeral homes to podcasts, to specialized companies, the obituary is finding a new home outside the newspaper, for better or worse.

While I would prefer that the obituary section remains in the physical newspaper of the past, this single source has allowed us to make key connections to death as old classmates start to appear on the page, and we begin to contemplate our own mortality.

With the loss of merely glancing over the obituary section as we make our way through the news, we lose the opportunity to catch when the John Doe we went to high school with but with whom we since have lost touch has passed away. We lose the chance to internalize the realizations at points in life when others start to pass at the same age we are or do not make it to the age that we have reached as we sit and read their obituary.

THE START OF SHRINKING OBITUARIES
Throughout the early 2000s, the decline of the print newspaper has been staggering. The first decade of the century brought with it the bankruptcy of numerous long-established newspapers in large metropolitan cities. These bankruptcies centered on the recent losses in revenue as a result of new competition with online sites like craigslist.com according to a study published in *Management Science*, which has cost the newspaper industry $5.4 billion between

2000-2007 exacerbated by the lack of buyers for the larger companies once revenue all but disappeared.[24] Advertising revenue for US newspapers fell from nearly $70 billion in 2000 to roughly $15 billion by 2015, and over the same period, the number of newspaper firms in the US dropped from 6,200 firms to just over 4,200. With this rapid decline in revenue, new strategies and sacrifices had to be developed and adapted. Many journalists and obituaries had to find a new place in the world. *The San Francisco Chronicle* avoided closing with deep concessions from employees, while the *Tucson Citizen*, Arizona's oldest paper, ceased publication altogether.

Newspapers faced a need to re-strategize their plan with some of the more successful surviving papers building their online pay-to-read subscribers, building educational publishing departments, and exploring other new and creative forms of diversification. This shift in corporate strategy also contributed to the forced cut back of sections like the obituaries to fulfill a strategic business model.

Over the same period, the cost of a standard "traditional" 4.5-inch obituary in the *Kansas City Star* jumped from less than $200 to roughly $450 by 2020, according to a funeral director in the area. Second-day printings of a four-line service announcement, which states basic abbreviated information, jumped from approximately $25 to nearly $90 over the same period.

---

24   Robert Seamans and Feng Zhu, "Responses to Entry in Multi-Sided Markets: The Impact of Craigslist on Local Newspapers," (PDF). *Management Science*. 60 (2)(February 2014): 476–493, Accessed May 29, 2020.

"Simply put," wrote The Buffalo News owner Warren Buffett during this re-strategizing of the newspaper industry, "If cable and satellite broadcasting, as well as the Internet, had come along first, newspapers, as we know them probably, would never have existed." [25]

ADDRESSING THE ELEPHANT IN THE ROOM

With the subtle connections that come with identifying a person's life documented in an obituary, we start to chip away at our own aversion to the subject of death. We encounter the finite amount of time we have, and with it, the stresses that go unsaid and the plans that are left unplanned when we avoid the inevitable.

Some believe there is no reason to "rock the boat" on the subject of death without need, for fear of jinxing the idea. If we instead ease into the thought of dying with small hints like a glance at the obituary page, we stand to benefit far more, igniting thoughts about death and the value of our lives in small ways, little by little with each view.

This exposure allows us to ease into the conversation with ourselves, at our own pace, bringing the benefits of lower stress and lower death anxiety once we confront these ideas.

Encountering death in small ways, like reading a somber or comical obituary, exposes the reader to the subject of an eventual end. A simple search online of comical obituaries

---

25   John Morton, "Buffeted: Newspapers Are Paying the Price for Short-sighted Thinking". American Journalism Review. Archived from the original on 2008-10-10. (October–November 2007), Retrieved 2020-02-10.

will produce several results that range from total fabrications to harshly accurate portrayals. The obituaries highlight those who have chosen to share their obituary information in a way that eased the hurdles present confronting death. In some ways, the very act of confronting the idea of death can promote increased mindfulness, expanded self-analysis, and deeper contemplation.

A DYING ART

We might also ask ourselves that if we move away from obituaries that are written in newspaper format, a format that is written by professionals in most cases who have been taught to do so, will we be left without a guide to draw from, or are we instead losing of the art of obituary writing entirely?

With the transition from the printed editions of newspapers to online resources outside the newspaper comes the added challenge of prioritizing the search for materials that once filled a section of the newspaper. The convenience of a newspaper delivered to our front porch or seen at every newsstand daily, which featured an Obituary Section, is something we may not experience again with the same ease until the world adapts to a digital lifestyle. You may ask yourself: if John Doe died and you were without your printed hometown newspaper, would you know about it? Or would he know if something had happened to you?

CHAPTER SIX

LEARNING FROM THE END

What is it that makes a life stand out? What is the secret or behavior we could learn from others that came before us that cause those around us to say, "Wow, what a life!"

The insights and secrets about how to live a "good" life can be learned from the generations who came before us. Cautionary tales about avoiding egg salad sandwiches from hot truck stop vending machines or sage advice about negotiating salaries can be gathered from those who have encountered the same path before and have learned wisdom from real-life experiences. We can learn a lot from a life well-lived, and what better resource to efficiently learn about some of the notable highlights of a person's life than an obituary?

What if we started to set goals in life from the wisdom we gain from generations that came before us? What if we then set up our own goals in life to be acknowledged, only after we have ended our time on earth?

With goals extended far past a point where we have control over how these goals are interpreted, they might make us strive to make the things we do and the decisions we make leave a lasting testament of the life we lived. Living this way, we could hope to teach others the lessons we leave behind but are no longer here to teach.

Lakshmanan, or Lux Narayan, a kind-looking, lightly bearded man, came to the United States several years ago and has continued his habit of continuous learning in various areas, from origami and molecular gastronomy to stand-up and improv comedy. In one of his stand-up routines at the Comedy Cellar's Village Underground, he even joked that he had a solid grasp of call center English in his first years in the US when joking with friends about the peculiarities of speech.[26] From his office on Wall Street within view of the famous Charging Bull sculpture by Sicilian artist Arturo Di Modica, which has become a favorite target for those looking to get some extra likes on a picture while visiting the Big Apple, he wondered why so many would prefer such a spot.

Lux began watching those who gathered around this statue, noting in his stand-up routine that roughly half of those he observed taking these pictures with the bull statue seemed to choose an odd place to stand. After observing the crowd as he ventured into his office every day, it became evident that the crowd seemed to favor posing with the rear end of the statue and its prominent features with surprising enthusiasm.

---

26 Lux Narayan, "Lux Narayan's debut set at the Comedy Cellar." Posted February 20, 2017. Video, 7:55.

"Why would they do this?" Lux asked himself. The possible answer was: "Facebook economics. They do it for the likes."

As part of his morning routine, Lux enjoys eating scrambled eggs and looking over the morning edition of *The New York Times*—more specifically, the obituary section. In his Ted-Talk, Lux states, "What I learned from 2,000 obituaries... My wife understandably thinks I'm morbid to begin my day with scrambled eggs and a 'Let's see who died today.'"[27]

After reading countless obituaries of interesting and famous people who made lasting impacts on the world, Lux wondered whether there was a commonality among these people.

That's the way Lux's brain works. Training first as an engineer then specializing in marketing as part of his MBA, drawing insights and data, led Lux first to co-found the short-lived Vembu Technologies, an online data backup company. He then co-founded and headed his company Unmetrics, a social media intelligence company based in New York and India that focused on future insights marketers can derive from data.

The morning paper provides so much information and data about the world around us. Lux stated in his Ted Talk, "But if you think about it, the front page of the newspaper is usually bad news, and cues man's failures. An instance where bad news cues accomplishments is at the end of the paper in the obituaries."[28]

---

27 Lux Narayan, "What I Learned From 2,000 Obituaries," Filmed January 2017 at TEDNYC. Video, 6:00.

28 Ibid.

With a company full of friends and colleagues at his disposal, he thought, why not run an analysis of a large sample of obituaries form *The New York Times*? They could search for commonalities and insights that might shed light on some aspect of life that was perhaps being overlooked and counter the rest of the news in the paper.

So, that is just what he did. After asking favors and working during his downtime, Lux ran the immense task of analyzing two thousand editorial, non-paid obituaries over twenty months between 2015 and 2016.

What did Lux find? What did these two thousand lives teach us? First, they showed that the obituaries were 80 percent male, with a majority of those featured making their most significant contribution at roughly thirty-seven years of age and dying on average forty-four years later at eighty-one years old, with ages ranging from 19 to 113, as well as less than 5 percent of those featured dropping out of school or college. This statistic logically should shift as modernity and cultural shifts that have made the world a more diverse place came about as these new generations reached a point where they would need an obituary.[29]

After injecting the entire first paragraph, instead of just the headline descriptor, into their analysis, while using Natural Language Processing to omit filler words like *the, and, or,* they ran a word analysis. They then separated the obituaries into two categories: "Famous" (those with names that are recognizable household names like Muhammad Ali), and

---

29 Ibid.

"Non-famous" (individuals you may have never heard of outside of the featured obituary who still impacted the world).

In the Non-famous group, commonalities like the name *John* appeared heavily in the two thousand obituaries along with the word *help*. With this data, Lux said, "The exercise was a fascinating testament to the kaleidoscope that is life, and even more fascinating was the fact that the overwhelming majority of obituaries featured people, famous and non-famous, who did seemingly extraordinary things. They made a positive dent in the fabric of life. They helped."[30]

In the Famous group, the name *John* also came through in the top results. *Art, music, help,* and *work* also came through as frequent words. These were former stars and titans who you might know by name in your household, but still, many of the same words came through in their life review in the heading of their *NYT* editorial obituary.

The arts came to the surface of the analysis more than any other area; film, theater, literature, music, and art proved to be huge in the study. This begs the question: why are we so persistent in guiding our children toward professions in engineering, business, law, and medicine to be counted as successful?

One of the most important questions someone might want to ask themselves if they hope for the highest likelihood of being featured in a *New York Times* editorial obituary is this:

---

30   Ibid.

"How am I using my talents to help society?"

Lux posited an answer to the question with this newfound knowledge, "How am I using my talents to help society?" He co-founded the ShareMyCake Charitable Foundation, a non-profit that focuses on raising more generous children, a non-profit started by his wife that focuses on encouraging children to use their birthdays to channel monetary support toward a cause of their choosing. He also has taken to performing stand-up comedy, and he makes time every year for trekking in the Himalayas or scuba diving in tropical waters. Once he learns to fly, he hopes to spend more time off the land than on it.

"The most powerful lesson here is if more people lived their lives trying to be famous in death, the world would be a much better place," Lux concluded.[31]

---

31   Ibid.

CHAPTER SEVEN

MODERN NOTIFICATIONS

———

Most mornings, even before my alarm goes off, I'm awakened by a familiar sound: Ding. And then another. Ding. Before my feet even hit the floor, I have picked up my phone from my nightstand and begun to read the morning news. Let's face it: fewer people read the newspaper today than they did yesterday. In the technological world we live in, most of the information we encounter comes from an online source.

In today's world, we hear about news with a "ding" or a feed that populated our screen as a notification. We know instantly if someone liked a video we posted or if there was an earthquake on the other side of the globe. Large amounts of disparate information reach our screens constantly and the way we filter this information and peruse notifications may be more complicated than we give ourselves credit for.

Notifications are constant. They are new messages, posts, and tags from everyone, and no one. These small bits of information posted by the world around us carry news, both new and old, funny and sad, every day and odd.

We feel good and maybe even a twinge of excitement when we open one of our social media applications and see notifications waiting for us. They are things we care about, at least a little, most of the time. They help bring all the critical events of the recent past to the front and center. Some get a glance; others get a more in-depth look or an expanded read. On a good day "likes" rain down on everything we see; on other days, we are more reserved and enjoy our anonymous scrolling.

We get to be involved in everyone's life we choose to be, from lifelong friends to one-time acquaintances. All of them, for better or worse, are there. Often posts are joys and slight brags, but sometimes they serve as a way to vent or share sorrows. Whether we see these notifications as a numbered bubble that draws the eye, or via alarms, chimes/dings, red "unread" notifications in social media, and unread text messages, each is attached to something that will impact us. Usually, the impact is small, but sometimes, as many of us have learned, it can carry so much more.

According to an IDC Research study, "Within the first fifteen minutes of waking up, four out of five smartphone owners are checking their phones, and among these people, nearly 80 percent reach for their phone before doing anything else and 62 percent reach for it immediately after waking up."[32]

---

32   IDC Research, "Always Connected," An IDC Research Report, Accessed May 29, 2020.

This data was gathered as part of a study conducted as an online survey of 7,446 people sponsored by Facebook of eighteen to forty-four-year-old iPhone and Android smartphone owners in the United States. The findings go on to report that, on average, users spend more than an hour on social media sites each weekday and more than two hours Friday through Sunday.[33]

My habits are not much different, nor free from the highs and lows found on social media.

It was the middle of winter outside, and the winds that always found Mount Oread on cold days caught the bare branches of the trees on campus and drew my attention out the window. The cold air made even the moving trees feel still. The sunlight brought a warm glow to the limestone-clad campus, even in the midmorning hours. The light of my cell phone seemed to fill the dark corner of my room as I grabbed it from the charger, and as the numbers show us, most of us wake accompanied by the same glow of cellphone light in the modern world.

It was a groggy college morning as I stumbled through my dorm room, throwing on a shirt and sitting down in the oversized chair squeezed into my tiny room. I began my daily routine with a glance at my cellphone before getting ready for the day.

---

33 An IDC Research Report, "Always Connected," IDC Research, Accessed May 29, 2020.

First up, I checked my email. Nothing seemed to stand out while scrolling through the headlines. The typical group project back and forth and a few forwards of a cat with a funny caption overhead. Nothing was so important that it could not be handled later during a lecture.

Next up, social media. That will get the brain going. A quick scroll through Twitter was a good place to start. All seems well; a celebrity commented on this or that, a friend linked an odd news clip, and there was a far-out political post here and there. Again, nothing interesting enough to dive into came across the screen with each rapid scroll, each post addressed with partial attentiveness as I continued to wake up.

Facebook seemed like an excellent way to wrap things up before heading to the showers. My wall sprang to life with a click of the blue logo. Pictures of friends instantly populated my screen. A post from friends who had rebelled and gone out the night before came up and inspired closer examination. A quick zoom in and *yup, that's what I thought I saw.* That was a picture with the guy down the hall in the background. *I'm sure he will be untagging that one later. Yikes!* One index finger flick after another, the past days' highs and lows came across the screen. Another post about a group studying for a test brought the day's schedule to mind. I was not ready for that, yet I kept scrolling. Next, there was a status update from "In a Relationship" to "It's Complicated." *Must have been a rough night.* More of the expected pictures and posts, some happy, another scroll, some excited, another scroll, some vague continued to show up on the screen. Wait, what did that one say?

The world lost two great people last night. This Sucks. (5:13 a.m.)

That's not good, who posted it? Oh, a friend from high school. Must have been a family member, wonder who?

Another heavy scroll of the index finger sent still more skimmed posts across the screen.

Another post, Heaven gained two beautiful souls. Praying for their families. (5:37 a.m.)

Man, it must have been somebody back home.

It was just past 7:30 a.m.

A piece of small-town news always seemed to spread like wildfire, and Facebook only gave those of us out-of-town a glimpse at how far and fast news spread. *I wonder whose parents it could be.*

Another heavy scroll, another similar post, stopped on the screen.

Jake & Steph, at least you have each other. We'll miss you! Sending our prayers! (7:12 a.m.)

Wait a minute. Huh? Jake and Stephanie. That can't be right.

I'd seen them on campus Friday. I could see the profile right in front of me. We were connected as much as all of our other friends at that moment, by opposing ends of the screen. Our disconnection felt more real with the devastating news, and the shock that accompanied felt like I was one of the last to hear, when in reality it had only been a few hours. We are all so connected by our loose online connections, which makes it hard to comprehend that we also simultaneously are disconnected.

Soon I was drowning in the information that social media was only too willing to provide with efficiency. Looking at each of their profile pages and the messages that were posting by the minute, I knew it was true.

Two deaths had gone viral in our small community just a short ride down the road, the same roads that had been the site of the last moments of the same two friends' lives. The first members of our friend group from high school, the two who had always been the ones who would be together forever, had been in a car crash.

Among the feed of puppy pictures, memes, and pictures from high points of the weekend, I had learned that two of my friends were gone forever.

In this age of modern and instant notification, we receive most of our information from the mixed bag that is social media. We get to hear about the world around us in real-time and have a chance to receive the past at will. Sometimes an annoying ping is just too much, or a build-up of uninteresting notifications and messages has to be cleared. Still, in some cases, the constant scrolling brings information we will never really be ready to hear.

Being conscious of what is being shared both as a person posting, and as a person reading a post, allows us to start developing an internal gauge of the etiquette required for posting on social media in the tech generation.

CHAPTER EIGHT

THE REACH OF SOCIAL MEDIA

───

Imagine a world in which everyone you know, knows each other. A world where everyone had an equal connection with everyone else. Any of our connections could share a message with every single person you had ever known because they know each of them too. For good or bad, a message would have full saturation into our entire social network both online and in reality. This fully integrated world does not exist for us, however—and how could it? We all live full, rich, independent lives in which we meet different people and experience different things. Because of this, we become susceptible to some vulnerabilities in communication with our social network if we are not the ones sharing the message.

In a presentation entitled "The hidden influences of social media," Nicholas Christakisa, professor of social and natural sciences at Yale University, brought up the concept of the Widowhood Effect, the increased likelihood for a recently widowed person to die, and posited that this effect might not be restricted to our spouse.[34] It might not even be limited to pairs of people but likely has degrees of effects throughout our social networks.

This idea hit him when he was working as a hospice doctor at the University of Chicago. Nicholas was taking care of dying patients and their families in the South Side of Chicago, observing what happened to people and their families over the course of a terminal illness.

"I was studying the widowhood effect, which is a very old idea in the social sciences, going back 150 years, known as 'dying of a broken heart,'" he states in his TedTalk.[35] In the first year that follows a spouse's death, the risk of death can double.

In one particularly pivotal encounter in his formation of the expansion of the widowhood effect, Nicholas was helping a woman dying of dementia. In this instance, the woman's daughter happened to be the primary caregiver and was experiencing severe exhaustion as a result of the caregiving experience. As a result of the fatigue experienced from caregiving, the daughter's husband was also becoming sick from exhaustion.

While on a drive home, Nicholas received a phone call from the husband's friend. It was not a call of concern for the dying woman, or even a call asking for extra attention to help the daughter acting as the primary caregiver. The husband's

---

34   Felix Elwert and Nicholas Christakis. ""The Effect of Widowhood on Mortality by the Causes of Death of Both Spouses." *American Journal of Public Health*, 98(11), 2092–2098.

35   Nicholas Christakis, "The hidden influence of social networks," Filmed February 2010, video, 28:07.

friend was calling because he was depressed about what was happening to his friend. The call was coming from someone going through a hard time that was several degrees of separation away from the patient Nicholas was treating, a significant degree of social separation in most people's minds.

"I suddenly realized two very simple things: First, the widowhood effect was not restricted to husbands and wives. And second, it was not restricted to pairs of people," Nicholas recalled.[36] At this point, the intricate social networks we have started factor into the widowhood effect. The results of the connections that we have, both closely with family, and loosely with friends and acquaintances, are all subject to the ripple of what another person is experiencing. Some people in the network experience emotional responses, while others experience none at all when a person in the network dies.

When parts of our social circles are scattered to and fro from one friend group to the next, with many of these individuals and groups being completely isolated from each other not only by connections but by social networking platforms, it becomes easy to see the gaps in support systems.

What effects might these disconnects have concerning hearing about a death on social media?

"Not everyone has the same level of integration within their social network," Nicholas shared. "We know that some people are born shy, and some are born gregarious."[37]

---

36 Ibid.
37 Ibid.

Some people take time to connect their friends with each other to create a cohesive web of mutual connections, while others have distinct and separate groups of friends that are disparate from each other. The unification of friend groups is evident in people around us who integrate their work colleagues, their friends from college, and their family all into a connected group, establishing relationships in and among all the people in each group. At the same time, others prefer to separate these circles from one another, choosing to interact with each group or individual separately.

These gaps in the connection from one group to the next may be enough for a group, or *several* groups of people, to miss an announcement about funeral service times that are shared via friends and family members' social networks.

The disconnection among individuals that exists also creates an opportunity for what is called **Disenfranchised Grief**, grief that is unrecognized or acknowledged by our social norms and society. The presence of disenfranchised grief in the past may have been reserved perhaps for an ex-spouse, or the other half of a secret affair, individuals who would have been mourning a loss of a loved one but not received support in their grief by their surrounding community.

Disenfranchised grief may now have much broader implications as our lives and connections are shared with an ever-broadening group of people through social media. What might be a simple post to you, like pictures from a family hike or a candid shot taken as someone laughs at a joke during a dinner out with friends, might be a much more important connection point to someone else. This post could represent a heartfelt level of connection to one of your friends on social media. Each of our tweets, posts, and likes has the potential to make a stronger connection, one that could be unrecognized even by the person writing the post.

Complications might extend farther for someone with distinctly separated friend groups who could experience disenfranchisement simply because a family member does not know that a close friendship outside of the known friend groups existed. Disenfranchised grief brings with it a broader application in a time of infinite connections, leaving the door open for continued improvement about how information is broadcast so that essential relationships are reached in the future.

Your social network is different than the networks of your friends and family, which brings up an important question. How many people in your social network could potentially miss out on the fact that you died if family or friends do not have access to your social media connections or the contacts on your iPhone? It has become a point of contention.

MY PHONE IS LOCKED, AND I'M DEAD. WHO CAN GET ACCESS?

A phone that is locked by a password requires the passcode to gain access by the family. If you do not have the access code, the chances of accessing the deceased's phone become substantially more complicated, in some cases requiring court actions to access.

Some phones grant access via fingerprint, but a detail that is usually overlooked is that this requires a thermal trace or warm finger in most smartphones. While there have been cases where a phone has been unlocked by using the deceased person's fingerprints, this fails more often than not.

Once embalming occurs, the chances of any success plummet almost to zero as the fingertips usually take on a rigid or slightly pruned surface. This is a narrow window of opportunity as well, due to access to the finger being non-existent after the person is buried or cremated. I have never heard of an exhumation being conducted for a fingerprint, and I can imagine I never will. The implications of law enforcement using fingerprints postmortem have also caused this subject to go under the magnifying glass with new laws focusing on this privacy issue specifically.

Facial recognition has similar limitations. It is easy to imagine that when you are lying down flat in bed, some of your facial structures are affected due to the change in gravity. Even more of a change happens when you relax all of your facial muscles at the same time. A similar effect occurs when you are embalmed; the features are set in place. While it may be possible to use facial recognition to unlock a phone in some cases after death, I would not count on this being the case either. In all cases, legal protections to privacy exist, and it is essential to remember that you and your loved ones are entitled to these privacy rights even from each other.

CONNECTED TO EVERYTHING AND NOTHING

The extent of our social connections both in the real world and online via social media sites are intricate webs of connectedness. Some of these connections will have significant impacts on our lives, and some will incite small grief responses as though we are observing a hardship. Not all reactions to the loss of the many connections we have in this world will be the same.

A distant relationship dying may provoke a surprisingly large grief response within us. We also may not feel the death of a close family member with as many eternally visible cues as others. Grief is not predictable with any curtain accuracy, nor is who is affected by a loss. It is important to remember that each of us grieves differently and remind ourselves that some connections that we are unaware of in another person's life might be very meaningful. The small ways someone maintains that connection, be it a post or a photo, can make a big difference.

URNING THE ANSWER:

ASHES, WHAT ARE THEY REALLY?

———

Inevitably when the topic of cremation comes up, one of the most common responses lately has been:

"Have you seen that your ashes can be put in a thing that helps a tree grow? That's what I want."

While the intentions for sustainability, eco-consciousness, and pure practicality are spot on, filling some gaps in knowledge can change this from a good idea to a plan that delivers the desired results.

Let's start by breaking down the cremation process to give us a good idea of precisely what we are working with.

Are they really called ashes? In the funeral industry, the physical ashes that remain after cremation are known as *cremains,* a combination of the words *cremated* and *remains.* So, ashes, or cremains, are the tangible product that exists after a cremation. These are fragments that are swept out of the cremator (the large machine used to perform a cremation) after the cremation has taken place.

The cremation process begins with paperwork that is finalized in most states after death with a cremation authorization. Once all of the required documents are completed and approved, a rigid identification process of the body takes place.

The identification process usually involving placing a metal tag that will survive the cremation with the body that has matching numbers to the deceased's paperwork. During the wait, the body is kept in a temperature-controlled chilled room or refrigeration. At this point, the body is also examined for any potential dangers, such as a pacemaker that, if present, is removed. Pacemaker batteries tend to explode and damage the brick lining of the retort (the space in the cremator where the body is placed) while also posing a risk to the crematory operator.

The body then is moved from the cooled room or refrigeration and taken to a high-powered furnace referred to as a cremator. During this time, the body is placed in a rigid container, which ensures that only one body can fit into the retort at a time. This cremator is powered by propane or gas, operating at an average temperature of 1800 degrees Fahrenheit. The person operating this high-powered furnace in most states is often a certified crematory operator (CCO) like me and has gone through additional specialized cremation training programs.

The body is placed inside the chamber called a retort for roughly two hours, allowing the body to break down into dense bone material by the flame-heated chambers of the cremator, then cools down for nearly half an hour depending on the facility's equipment and procedures.

At this point, the bone fragments that remain in the retort are removed with a long-handled broom. During the removal of cremains from the retort, every effort is taken by the crematory operator to remove any remnants that exist, large or small. This effort to gather any remnants is undertaken to prevent the co-mingling of ashes since the same chamber will be used for the next cremation and so on. Since the chamber is not washed out or cleaned with anything other than the long-handled broom, a thorough sweeping is key in gathering all contents in the retort. At the same time, any surviving implanted materials, like a metal plate or an aluminum hip joint, are removed using a magnet and search of the cremains for recycling.

These implants often are recycled by companies explicitly established to serve the crematory and cemetery industries by recycling the metallic by-products of the cremation process.

Now that we know what happens to the human body during cremation and how the process works, we have reached the point when only bone fragments remain, some as small as a grain of sand, others still resembling pieces of bone. All of this is placed in a machine eloquently called a Pulverizer (think food processor, but for bones). This machine processes the differing sizes of bone fragments to a uniform consistency with the equivalency of course sand.

The average adult creates about five pounds of human cremains. These cremains take up a space of roughly two hundred cubic inches, which are placed in a container (a temporary urn) and returned to the family. Most often, this temporary urn is a plastic or cardboard container with a zip-tied plastic bag inside that holds the cremains before being placed in a permanent urn. Children's cremains range from a small thimble-sized amount for a premature birth, to amounts that grow as the child reaches maturity. Rarely does the weight of the person vary the amount of cremains. Instead, the amount of cremains is impacted more by bone density with height coming in at a close second.

Once the cremation is complete, we have reached the point of final disposition.

> *The Point of Final Disposition is the point at which someone's physical remains have reached a point of no return without extraordinary effort. In the context of burial, this occurs at the moment the casket is lowered into the ground in the cemetery. As far as most overarching government regulations are concerned, what you do with cremains following the cremation is the decision of the persons in charge, whether that is the next of kin or the "durable power of attorney with rights to disposition."*

* * *

DURABLE POWER OF ATTORNEY ASSIGNMENT

A quick aside that might prove helpful in future funeral arrangements concerns the assignment of a Durable Power of Attorney (DPOA), the person who is assigned to be in charge if you become incapacitated and unable to handle matters on your own. The role of the DPOA, in most cases, however, ends at death, meaning this person is not in charge of the funeral. Having the "rights to disposition" added is advisable when you have this legal document composed. The DPOA with rights to disposition allows the person you have assigned to be in charge of your medical decisions if you become unable to do so **and** the right to continue to be in charge of your funeral arrangements as well, which helps prevent any possible division regarding funeral planning between those who are left behind. Otherwise, this right is granted to your next of kin or divided among your children, and a majority decision is required to move forward in most states. If you think your funeral plans and wishes might be a point of contention among those you leave behind, assigning a DPOA with rights to disposition would be an advisable, wise, and legally binding means of preventing possible heartache.

* * *

Now the cremains are ready for temporary options like being displayed on a mantle or placed in scattering urns or permanent solutions like burial, scattering, or any number of uses that are meaningful to loved ones.

Many people, including me, find comfort in spending time in nature. Especially in a garden, on the banks of a picturesque body of water, or under the shade of a tree on a hilltop. It is no wonder that so many people are drawn to making this connection point with nature more permanent by choosing to bury or scatter their ashes in these places. The logic is there and what a special place for family to recall in a mental image or visit to feel a connection to you.

Since this is such a heartfelt and popular option, I have to wonder: are people getting what they actually want when they choose this path and does it deliver the desired results? Are the ashes that are being placed under a newly planted tree or bush beneficial to the plant? These are important points to consider when thinking about the long-term connections to places in nature that now have added meaning for your loved ones.

Essentially, cremains (ashes) are *dry calcium phosphates* with a small combination of minerals like *sodium* and *potassium*, which is the same for human cremains and pet cremains, both coming from the bone matter that remains.[38]

> *When it comes to gardening, will plants grow in a bulk amount of ashes? The unfortunate answer is: no.*

Unlike other nutrients that you place in your garden, ashes do not decompose as plant matter would. In fact, cremated remains may be harmful when placed in large amounts around plants and trees. While cremains contain many nutrients that plants need like calcium, phosphorus, and potassium, they also have a large amount of salt, or sodium, which is toxic for most plants. They lack essential micronutrients

---

38   Mary H. Dyer, "Planting in Cremation Ashes – Are Cremation Ashes Good for Plants," Gardening Know How, Accessed May 29, 2020.

essential to plant growth, like zinc and manganese. Large amounts of calcium, which is in large part what cremains are, deplete the nitrogen in the soil while having a high pH level, which can also affect plant growth.

Before you start digging someone's ashes up from your garden or changing the plan for your cremains all together, STOP! Mixing small amounts of cremains into the soil is relatively harmless to the health of the plants or trees in your garden.

Urns are available that claim to be composed of rebalanced soil that will counteract the adverse effects of a large volume of ashes near a plant. Most of these urns also have seedlings or seeds integrated into the outer layers that could grow after burial, providing some ease of mind if this is the option that suits you.

You should think about several things before associating someone's cremains with a particular tree or plant:

- Plants die too! You should ask yourself:
  - Will there be an emotional response or resurgence that occurs when this plant or tree dies?
  - Will this be akin to losing this person again or for the final time?
  - If so, that is something to consider if you select this path.

- Are you good at caring for existing plants or trees?
  - You might have an emotional connection to this plant and feel a need to continue to care for the plant to

maintain a relationship with the person who has died if it has a direct association with someone's ashes.

- If you like the thought of going to the garden to have a connection but lack a "green thumb," as they say, you might consider alternatives like mixing the cremains into concrete for a bench or decorative feature in the garden instead.

• Is this plant or tree in a place you can visit for as long as you want to?
  - Planting a tree or bush in a private garden is very convenient, but if the need arises to sell the house, it may become difficult to visit.
  - Alternatively, if ashes are associated with a tree, trees grow quite large, making it harder to relocate them.
  - Will you be affected if the person who buys your house cuts down the tree?
  - If these are points of distress for you, will making a plaque alongside the ashes that can be moved to a future garden or cemetery instead if the need arises be an acceptable point of remembrance for you?

As long as ashes are integrated into a garden healthily, using the opportunity as a meaningful way for family and loved ones to remember a loved one in a caring way, the potential options are endless. It is advisable, however, to be observant and be aware of the possible presence of an intense emotional connection to a specific tree or plant that some friends or family may have. Weighing this knowledge when considering placement and utilization of cremains in a garden as a final path can provide a mindful and desirable resolution for all those involved and for their mental wellbeing in the future.

IT'S ABOUT MORE THAN THE ASHES...

Are cremains beneficial for trees? No, but ashes are what is left of our loved ones after cremation. Treating them in a way that creates meaning and a mode of remembrance to those who have lost someone they care for is priceless. If done in the right way and for the proper purposes, the integration of cremains into a garden can be a meaningful final resting place that is valued by those we leave behind.

I know that if my ashes are scattered around a fruit tree in the garden, that tree will grow and be cherished. After nature has decided that fruit tree has produced its final fruit and completed its course of life, it too will return to the earth and nourish other plants, trees, and flowers. In a way, the romantic vision of the natural cycle of Mother Nature carries a special meaning for those who I, unfortunately, have to leave behind when my time comes. And I am okay with that.

Our experiences with death can be a profoundly personal and meaningful experience. The way we encounter the ceremony as a diverse community can affect each person in attendance and carry unique meanings with each of us into the future. Variables in how we conduct ceremonies or the path we choose for our remains can have a lasting impact on those we leave behind.

"No one is actually dead until the ripples

they cause in the world die away."

—TERRY PRATCHETT

CHAPTER NINE

FROM VISIBLE
TO USABLE

———

Over the past few decades, many new and forward-thinking ideas have come to light as possible future mainstream modes of disposition. Some are geared toward minimal environmental impact. Others try to create lasting connections to the living. Many try to cater to a wide range of modern ideas and desires for a choice in final disposition. As more alternatives become available and cultural trends shift and evolve, options that are more meaningful and individualized to a person's life will become more accessible. These changes will not be without obstacles. As new technologies are introduced, large religious and cultural organizations and groups will need time to consider the changes in their own context.

One of the key motivators behind our choices for our funeral is the views or the religious denomination we follow. Even within religions, different preferences exist around burial as opposed to cremation, with different preferences in one sect of a given religion to the next. World religions and denominations, including Judaism, Lutheranism, Mormon, Christian Science, Methodism, Islam, Episcopalian, Greek Orthodox, Baptist, Jehovah's Witness, Wiccan, Buddhism, Hinduism, Atheism, and many others all offer unique thoughts on what should be done with our bodies after death, with countless traditions and time-tested practices that go hand in hand with their beliefs.

Some have a very open view of the choices you want for your burial or cremation, and others prefer adherence to existing practices and beliefs. While many options continue to become available, their adaption from a religious point of view can take some time. It is essential not only to consider what factors will influence your funeral but the existence of opportunities for additional meaningful and spiritual moments. For some, these added sentiments come with the integration of religious traditions and practices.

Many religions are making changes that carry new opportunities for their followers. As a result of the Second Vatican Council, also referred to as Vatican II, members of the Catholic Church worldwide gained access to a new form of burial reserved for exceptional circumstances before the mid-1960s. Since then, cremation has grown to one of two popular types of final dispositions in the Western world. More recently, the Church of Jesus Christ of the Latter Day Saints has begun allowing cremation as an option under some provisions.[39] The escalation of cremations over the last half-century can

---

39 Do Latter-day Saints practice cremation? "Cremation is a custom in various parts of the world, Do Latter-day Saints practice it?" The Church of Jesus Christ of the Latter-Day Saints, Accessed May 29,2020.

be attributed to numerous causes and trends, passing the prior predominant mode of disposition as the most selected choice in how we spend eternity: burial.

Let's look at some of the opportunities coming into the mainstream as new technologies and products come online and are readily available.

USEABLE REMEMBRANCE

DNA SAMPLING

One growingly popular request that has become available before final disposition may be vital in realizing a new connection and the means of a lasting legacy between the living and deceased. Usable *DNA hair and blood sampling* that is taken post mortem, before preparations of the body, bridges the gap between legacy and usability. After gathering DNA samples from a loved one, the possible uses for these materials become numerous.

These uses can give insights with in-depth genetic testing, which allows access into ancestral links, family medical history, and many other future testing opportunities that leave a *usable* memorialization of the person who has passed away. DNA sampling can be a valuable continuation of an immense amount of genetic knowledge to those we leave behind. This genetic knowledge can now live on in addition to current memorialization options, like a *visible* urn or headstone.

ANATOMICAL DONATION

Many individuals choose to donate their physical remains as an Anatomical Donation. These cadavers are then used for medical training to scientific research. Many academic and research-oriented hospitals have Willed Body Programs designed to aid in making this an option that is available to you. If this is an option that appeals to you, please do your research. No two programs are the same and what you have in mind when you think of donating your body for research might not be in line with the program you are choosing. Ask questions. What research will be done with my body? Can I designate what research can and cannot be done with my body? Will this research be done in your facilities? Do you ever sell excess cadavers to other facilities? What will happen to my body after it has completed its use? Will my family receive my ashes when my body is eventually cremated? Will any of my organs, like my brain, be retained and used for research after my body has been cremated and returned to my family? **If you have a concern or question, ASK.** If an answer is not given or is not to your satisfaction, seek out other donation opportunities. Just because it is an anatomical "gift" does not mean you have to give up your say on what is done with your body.

GREEN BURIAL

The grass may literally be greener in some cases. Green burials are a growing trend in today's ecologically conscious world. As high-density and rural populations both move to take steps in their daily lives to make a smaller impact on Mother Earth, some are choosing to continue their efforts past the end of their lives.

A green burial is a burial designed and planned to create the smallest possible impact on the environment through the omission of preparations of the body like cremation or embalming while stepping away from the use of traditional metal or highly constructed caskets and burial vaults. These individuals instead select cloth shroud wrappings or purely natural wood or organic material casings, like wood or bamboo, in conjunction with a minimally marked and natural growth gravesite marker.

Green burials come in a wide range of choices and levels of adherence with many ways to personalize the process, allowing you to still partake in traditions and products that are important to you.

DIGITAL TOMBSTONES

A Slovenian cemetery is experimenting with weatherproof and vandal-proof "Digital Tombstones" that depict pictures and videos with the potential to link to smartphone applications for interactive experiences.[40] The innovations taking place with these digital tombstones in Pobrezje Cemetery, which sits on the outskirts of Maribor, Slovenia's second-largest city, might start to be used worldwide sooner rather than later.

While most new technologies have a starting price that is far above the current options, the estimated cost of 3,000 Euros offered by the manufacturer, Bioenergija, is in line with many of the headstone options that currently exist. The

---

40 "World's First Digital Tombstone – From Maribor Slovenia!" Slovenian Australian Chamber of Commerce. Published Jun 9, 2017.

integrative possibilities of a digital headstone truly showcase the innovations and social connectivity of the modern world.

Imagine walking through a cemetery and being able to discover the life story of the person buried before you. With linkability and message integration, how we remember those who have come before us might be more of an interactive experience in the future than it was in the recent past.

PET FUNERALS

In a modern technological world, many of our connections and communications with those around us happen at a distance. In many cases, the only in-person interaction we have that is constant is the one we have with our pets. They are there when we leave and waiting when we come home.

It is no surprise that the pet care industry is continually breaking yearly sales records as we care for one of the most consistent in-person interaction points we have in today's world. The same growth has occurred in how we care for our pets after they die. An elevated level of care for our pets' funerals is not a new idea.

The Hartsdale Pet Cemetery in Hartsdale, New York, just a short drive from New York City, opened its gates in 1896. Ever since, the hills that make up the Hartsdale Pet Cemetery have filled with the monuments of faithful companions and family pets, serving as the final resting place to more than eighty thousand pets.[41]

---

41   "Our History," Hartsdale Pet Cemetery. Accessed May 29, 2020

Cremation has become a preferred mode of disposition used for pets on a national scale, with new options like Aquamation, or water cremation, becoming available in some regions. Traditional human funeral homes, veterinarian practices, and stand-alone pet crematory and cemeteries all offer services that are geared specifically to our pets. Some states and cemeteries have even moved to make it easier to be interred side by side with your furry companion in "togetherness resting places" when the time comes to be reunited.

CREATIVELY SCATTERING ASHES

Many families select to display the ashes of their loved one in an urn on the mantel before eventually burying or scattering the ashes in a cemetery, lake, or other meaningful location. As can be imagined by most, if you do not own the land that you intend to scatter someone's ashes on, you need permission to do so. This also is the case for public waterways, which are owned by the federal government. In many cases, finding who to ask permission from could be a strenuous or exhaustive and sometimes fruitless endeavor, but these obstacles do not stop individuals from proceeding with their plans.

A 2018 *Wall Street Journal* article addressed what some families choose to do with their loved one's ashes. In the piece, entitled "Disney World's Big Secret: It's a Favorite Spot to Scatter Family Ashes," Erich Schwartzel shared some interesting information about one storybook scattering location: "Disney employees clean up scattered remains about once a month after visitors sneak in ashes to dispense at Cinderella's castle or various rides and attractions." When you start to think about it, that some people would like to have their ashes scattered at a place that held great family memories full of joy and togetherness is no surprise. Who else could do a better Donald Duck impression than Dad, after all? The stealthiness is admirable, but it is worth mentioning that getting permission is the most legal path to take even if, when scattered efficiently, the ashes are unidentifiable moments after they are scattered.

Some pertinent advice on the subject of scattering ashes can prove to be helpful if the need should arise for you that might bear repeating if you have prior knowledge on the subject already. The ashes from a cremation are different than the light, airy ashes one might find in a fireplace. Ashes, or cremains, as you have learned, are more granular with the consistency of sand, meaning that if you were to pour them out of a container, they would fall to the ground and create a small pile. If you broadcast them from the urn in a sweeping motion, the small granular pieces would be dispersed over the chosen area and be unrecognizable in the same instant.

One story, however, might prove to be a valuable lesson for the future. Some time ago, a rancher passed away and chose to be cremated, with the request that his ashes be scattered over their extensive ranch. In this way, he could be one with the land he had worked and loved forever and fulfill a full circle of life. The sons, one of which was an active pilot, thought there were few better ways to satisfy their father's wish than to scatter his ashes over a large part of his land while flying over the ranch. On a bright sunny day that showcased the beauty of the ranch, the sons took to the air. As they leveled out in their small propeller plane over their destination, approaching the edge of their property, they slid open the side window of the aircraft and began to scatter their dad's ashes.

As it would turn out, Dad was not going to go so easy and caught the incoming wind, filling the cabin with the dust that accompanies the granular mix of cremains that fell from the window of the plane. As they landed, the two sons and the plane's cabin were covered in a layer of Dad's ashes punctuated by the trails of tears of laughter on each of their cheeks. While the two sons thought of this occurrence as a fitting final rebellious act of their late father, they had succeeded in large part in the act of scattering their father's cremains over a large section of his ranch, learning a valuable lesson in the meantime.

When scattering ashes, make sure the wind is blowing away from you unless you would like a similar final embrace as the two men in the plane, or akin to a scene immortalized in cinema in *The Big Lebowski* (1998). The scene depicts a moment when "the dude," played by Jeff Bridges, and Walter Sobchak, played by John Goodman, scatter their bowling teammate Donny's (Steve Buscemi) ashes from a Folger's Coffee tin along the coast of California only to have the coastal winds blow the ashes back onto them, covering the dude from head to toe.

EVOLVING CEREMONIES

Along with the many evolving aspects of the funeral, likewise many new ceremonies honor the dead with growing popularity, some taking place before death occurs. The social acceptance of creativity surrounding funerals is much more accepted now than in the past. This has opened up the possibility for funerals to take on new or preferred tones to the traditional funeral. Now a funeral can carry the tone of a celebration of a life lived or even celebrate the life of someone still living.

LIVING WAKE

Some more death-positive individuals are choosing to attend their funeral before their death, by holding a "living wake" that offers family and friends a chance to say goodbye. These ceremonies can be held on a small scale at home with a small group of friends and family, or on par with a traditional funeral service in a funeral home or chapel. Some choose to have a full service with songs, eulogies, an (empty) casket, and reception to fully experience their funeral. For some, this creates added value and sentiment in having an idea of what will happen once they are gone, thus easing their uncertainties about the services they want and allowing them to make adjustments to their funeral plans.

CELEBRATIONS OF LIFE

Opening up the traditional Western funeral ceremonies that include wakes, visitations, and funerals to event planners, new activities, and speakers is becoming more popular. These events can occur at a much later date and serve as a way to celebrate the life and legacy of the person who has passed away. These ceremonies can be held in addition to a prior service that mourns the loss of the loved one or as a more cost-effective and practical option for some families.

Companies like Kaathy are beginning to offer additional event planning opportunities as an aid to planning at a funeral home. According to Kaathy.com, they are "the first of its kind online funeral planning platform that bridges the gap between funeral planners and the families to simplify the planning process."[42]

New opportunities exist to host any event you have in your mind, with professionals who can help make them happen or offer helpful advice.

LIVESTREAMING FUNERAL CEREMONIES

From wakes to burials, some funeral homes are adapting to the age of technology with new options that allow family members and friends the possibility of attending a funeral, visitation, and sometimes burial of someone who has passed away from a distant location via camera and various levels of connection to the services. Some firms are offering web links that connect to a video feed and other firms are utilizing meeting software like Skype, Zoom, Live Stream, Facebook Live, or many others. The ability now exists for family and friends who would have needed to undertake an extraordinary effort to attend a funeral. Whether hospitalized, home-bound, incarcerated, or in a distant country, the ability to view a funeral service now exists in a way that has never been more feasible.

---

42   "Home Page," Kaathy, Accessed June 1, 2020.

RETURN OF HOME FUNERALS

A current movement has expressed interest in making it more accessible to return to a funeral practice widely practiced before the 1950s in North America. Some individuals are choosing and finding deeper meaning in conducting their funeral in a family home. Home funerals can integrate many different choices in the service and visitation if held in the family home. In some cases, the family exclusively hosts those who attend the funeral. In contrast, others prefer to utilize a funeral home that simply conducts the visitation and funeral service in the family home. These services can include a prolonged period immediately following a death during which those close to the deceased can wash and dress the body and spend time before any services are performed. Home funerals can be performed with varying levels of aid and preparation in conjunction with a funeral home or crematory, depending on where you live in the country and your family's preferences.

CREATING A FAMILY CEMETERY

In some scenarios and locations, the opportunity to establish a family cemetery on land currently owned by the family is a possibility that creates additional meaning. A family cemetery creates a family-centric location that is easily accessible and meaningful to a family, creating a place to memorialize and remember a loved one or loved ones. While this is dependent upon local laws and ordinances, with enough preplanning and arrangement, this and many options can become available to a wide range of people across the country.

Usually, this option is more readily available in rural settings. Considering the future implications of establishing a family cemetery, however, is advisable. Ideally, a cemetery located at the top of a hill or in the middle of a field within walking distance of a house are picturesque options. However, considerations of future accessibility and resale of the land are worthwhile. One of the long-term suggestions addressing future concerns regarding access would be to locate this cemetery at a corner or edge of the given property near an existing road. This placement will allow future visits to be unobstructed by future landowners. Allowing the small piece of land used for a cemetery to be easily sectioned off from the larger plot of land will enable the family to maintain ownership of the cemetery.

The numerous ways to express and memorialize those we have lost allow each individual and family to have the ability to find the options that bring the most comfort and meaning to them.

CHAPTER TEN

HOW WILL YOU
SPEND ETERNITY?

―――

INNOVATIVE ADAPTIONS AND ALTERNATIVES
TO BURIAL AND CREMATION

Some states have legalized additional options already, while new conceptions are being made available around the world. Many new options are already in practice and even more are in development, meaning that the future may hold the right choice for you.

Whether proposed or already being slowly introduced to some areas, the diverse new options for burial may seem odd to some but may offer a comforting end to others. With growing use, more and more of these options will begin to enter mainstream use with time in some cases. Some may change greatly from country to country or state to state, but by merely discussing the option, you now have a jumping-off point to research and possibly encourage the option that seems right to you to be brought to your area or that legislation be introduced to make it possible.

ALKALINE HYDROLYSIS
(AQUAMATION OR WATER CREMATION)

Aquamation is a non-fire and greener alternative to cremation. Instead of flames, alkaline hydrolysis uses a specialized
machine that utilizes heated water and an alkali solution that
accelerates natural decomposition, under pressure and movement, after which the remains are processed in the same way
that occurs following a cremation. The alkaline hydrolysis
process produces around one and a half times the cremains
that are available following a cremation. This option is currently available in several states across the United States, with
shipment options available if you need it before your state
makes it locally possible.[43]

HUMAN COMPOSTING

With the passing of legislation in the State of Washington
in 2019, under close monitoring from other interested states
across the nation, the ability to choose to be composted as
a mode of disposition is now a legal option. Human composting has developed using two diverging processes, 1) a
whole-body composting process, 2) a composting after the
refinement process. Both methods use specialized bacterial
accelerant and natural heat to accelerate decomposition.
Composting presents an ecologically friendly solution to
reducing the impact and material waste of current burial
and cremation options. Though this is a new option, new
facilities are in development and may soon become available
through a local funeral home near you.

---

43 "Our Process," Aquamation, Accessed on May 29, 2020.

POMESSION

According to the KFDA Journal:

> Pomession is a process that was proposed by a Swedish scientist in 2015 to freeze-dry the body with liquid nitrogen and then subject it to intense vibration to break it into powder. The powder is then passed through a metallic separator to remove metal pieces, such as fillings and screws. The amount of powder remaining after the process is about the size of a potato bag. It is touted as being environmentally friendly. The body is broken down and turned into human soil allegedly within six to eighteen months of burial. The process has only been used on animals in Europe and has yet to be tested on humans.[44]

OPEN-AIR FUNERAL PYRE

Also referred to as open-air cremation, this option is available for a few people in the United States. As part of one of the world's oldest cremation traditions, a body is placed upon a structure packed with flammable material and ignited. The pyre burns at a very high temperature that reduces the human body and combustible material to a few pounds of rough ashes.

This mode of disposition was traditionally used by many cultures and religions, including Hinduism, Sikhism, and Vikings. A group in Colorado, the Crestone End of Life

---

44 Pam Scott, "A Word from the Executive Director," *KFDA Journal 80*, no.8 (September/October 2019): 4.

Project, has researched and obtained the proper permissions and permitting to create a permanent cement funeral pyre structure to preform open-air cremations, performing around twelve cremations a year.[45]

As part of a dignified process, the deceased is wrapped in a shroud and placed atop the pyre. During the placement ceremony, individuals have the option to put fragments of juniper branches on top of the body as part of the final viewing. Some share goodbyes, memories, or moments of silence while the juniper branches create a mound of flowers, branches, and greenery over the shrouded body. After the pyre is set ablaze, a ceremony of songs and prayers, depending on preferences, is conducted. Some take this opportunity to reflect, staying for hours to watch the fire as the sun sets in the distance.

Plan far in advance for this option to allow for restrictions and pre-planning that enable participation in this practice.

This is the perfect opportunity to remind you that you can inject any practice into almost any ceremony that has some degree of meaning to you. If you feel it would be beneficial to have everyone who wishes to place a flower in the casket or grave, or if you would like to give people a chance to place notes on a casket before burial or cremation, you can do so. If burning incense or candles has a meaning to you, brainstorm how this might be integrated into the ceremony as you plan the funeral with the funeral home staff and religious

---

45   "Crestone End-of-Life Project," Informed Final Choices, Accessed May 29, 2020.

figure. Nearly every funeral ceremony in every different church across the world is slightly different in some way, no matter how traditional the service. I can tell you this for a fact from firsthand experience. So, if something stands out as meaningful to you, you might creatively integrate it into your own services.

NEW PLACES TO SPEND ETERNITY

Alternatives to cemeteries make it possible for the lifelong adventurer to remain adventurous for all of eternity—well, sort of. While many of these offerings require pre-planning and tend to be costly, they are readily available to those who seek them out. You can explore these options personally or with the help of your local funeral home.

BURIAL FORESTS

In response to concerns over the land use of cemeteries and eco-responsibility, some companies have started promoting the idea of burial forests, forests that exist for the burial of ashes. Each burial takes place under a designated tree without the use of an obtrusive marker. Some burial forests having an end goal of being donated and earmarks for permanent preservation once capacity has been reached, with many of these forests utilizing lands found at the border of existing protected forests. Someone has the opportunity to select a large growth tree by size and age, with increasing cost for more mature selections, to serve as the natural marker of their cremation interment location. Each tree in the forest is reserved exclusively for one person in perpetuity, with the option of additional payments for the right to add other family members under the same tree. Essentially, this option is designed to make available cremation burial plots designed to fund forest preservation of the lands used.

BURIAL PODS

One company, Capsula Mundi, promotes the cycle of natural transformation for a burial pod design. "It's an egg-shaped pod, an ancient and perfect form, made of biodegradable material, where our departed loved ones are placed for burial. Ashes will be held in small egg-shaped biodegradable urns while bodies will be laid down in a fetal position in larger pods," Capsula Mundi's website states.[46] This positioning will be possible because rigor mortis happens at differing durations after death depending on the individual or circumstances around the death; after this period passes the body becomes malleable again and could be placed in the fetal position required for burial in the capsule.

"The Capsula" as Capsula Mundi refers to their pod, "will then be buried as a seed in the earth. A tree, chosen in life by the deceased, will be planted on top of it and serve as a memorial for the departed." From here, it is presumed family and friends will care for the tree for posterity, solidifying the legacy of the person and their connection with the earth. While it would increase the forest-like appearance of cemeteries that allowed for this option, several other aspects should be considered.

---

46 "Capsula Mundi, Life never stops," Capsula Mundi. Accessed May 29, 2020.

If the tree was struck by lightning, as many trees are, or suffered a termite infestation, would this be traumatic to those who are left behind? When choosing this plan, it might be advisable to lay out a plan for the future that includes replacement of the tree or letting the tree take its natural course of life, accepting the fact that one day the tree will be gone too.

ORBITING IN OUTER SPACE

SpaceX launched 152 cremated remains on a Falcon Heavy rocket. The "Funeral Flights" were arranged by a company called Celestis, offering spaces for $5000 for one gram of "participant" ashes.[47] (The average person's cremains weigh roughly five pounds or over 2250 grams.) Other options include launch to space and return to earth for future burial, being launched into earth's orbit, being launched to lunar orbit or surface, or becoming a voyager and be launched into deep space. These individuals, or at least a gram of them in some cases, will spend eternity in the void of space. As this option becomes more available, we have to wonder how long it will be until we have the opportunity to be buried on the moon or farther?

Unfortunately, I'm going to have to burst your bubble if you hoped to be the first person buried on the moon. That honor belongs to Eugene Shoemaker, who is still the only person buried on the moon. The late scientist who died in a car crash in 1997 is still the only person whose remains have been sent to the moon. Shoemaker's name is most

---

47   "Space Memorial Destinations," Celestis, Accessed June 1, 2020.

recognizable from the famed Comet, Shoemaker-Levy 9, which hit Jupiter in 1994. The comet, which Shoemaker discovered with his wife Carolyn and David Levy, was remarkable because it marked the first time humans were able to witness a planetary collision firsthand. The crash got so much press attention that a small town in Wyoming set up an intergalactic landing strip to welcome any potential refugees from Jupiter, and Shoemaker became a household name during the press coverage.

Aboard a NASA Lunar Orbiter Prospector Shoemaker's ashes made history. On July 31, 1999, the mission ended when NASA deliberately crashed the craft on the surface of the moon, taking Shoemaker with it, and making him the first and only person to be buried off-world.[48]

His ashes were carried aboard the NASA orbiter in a polycarbonate capsule provided by Celestis. It had been wrapped in a piece of brass foil, laser-etched with his name and life dates over an image of the Hale-Bopp Comet, an image of Arizona's Meteor Crater, where he had trained the Apollo astronauts, and a quote from Romeo and Juliet.[49]

TRANSFORMED INTO DIAMONDS

Human ashes or hair can now be engineered by turning the carbon into diamonds using a specialized machine and roughly half a cup of ashes or hair. These diamonds are physically and chemically identical to natural diamonds and are a

---

48 Eric Grundhauser, "Eugene Shoemaker Is Still the Only Man Buried on the Moon," *Atlas Obscura*, Published October 22, 2018.

49 Grunderhauser, "Eugene Shoemaker."

beautiful means of remembrance for a loved one. Be advised, however, that like diamonds from a store, this is not the most economical option.

Starting prices can range from three to five thousand dollars to fifty thousand dollars, with most taking over seven months to make.[50] Prices fluctuate with the selection, but the end product will forever sparkle as a diamond.

SMART LIBRARY COLUMBARIUMS

Shinjuku Rurikoin Byakurengedo, a spaceship-shaped building in Tokyo, lets you summon the ashes of a loved one with the swipe of a card, feeling more like a smart library than a cemetery.[51] A machine transports the ashes from a large underground storage vault via a conveyor belt to a viewing room.

The Ruriden Byakurengedo Columbarium is another option for cremated remains that contains illuminated buddhas that line the walls of a room, each associated with an individual's remains. This individual can be queued up via a nearby computer, after which the associated buddha illuminates in white light. In contrast, the other buddhas continue their slow transition of colored illuminations in shades of greens, blues, and red. The creative display offers a solution and connection point of technology and innovative solutions that also address land scarcity.

---

50 "One-of-a-kind, just like them." Eterneva, Accessed May 29, 2020.
51 Shiyu Song, "Architecture of Afterlife: Future Cemetery in Metropolis," (Doctoral Thesis, University of Hawai'i at Manoa, 2017).

In Oakland, California, a columbarium called Chapel of the Chimes, which is a large building with library-like rooms, has a unique way of displaying the remains of those inurned in their facility. Instead of ashes being placed in urns behind a stone or glass panel, as is the case in most columbariums, the Chapel of the Chimes places ashes in sealed "books" (urns) on shelves. Imagine the lessons we could learn from this library of souls if we had instant access to their life's work or a link to their digital remains.

MEMORIAL REEF

You could select to have your cremains mixed with a specialized reef ball material that is used in creating memorial reefs that can serve as a habitat for sea life. Other options exist that integrate reef and coral starts with an urn designed for this distinctive purpose. If diving or a life at sea are ideal ways to spend eternity for you, this may be your chance to be a part of the sea and rebuild a reef.

TATTOO INTEGRATION

A small amount of cremated remains can be mixed with the ink used in a tattoo to create a lasting, ever-present, and personal remembrance. This option requires a very small amount of ashes and many say that it gives added importance to the tattoo every time they see it.

WEARABLE ASHES

Many options allow you to integrate a fingerprint or a small portion of ashes into jewelry that can be worn as a heartfelt memorial to the person who has passed. Many choose to maintain a small token of those who have passed that allows for a small degree of constant contact offering comfort to them in their times of grief.

Ashes can be integrated into a wide range of products from ceramics and paintings to personal massagers and vinyl records. The versatility of ashes allows for endless opportunities to create items of remembrance that are important to the people who cherish them.

FUTURE PLACES TO SPEND ETERNITY

FLOATING CEMETERY

In response to limitations in urban and high-density cities and countries, one architectural option conceived for Hong Kong is a floating cemetery.[52] This cemetery would dock at strategic spots for holidays of remembrance then return to less central and commercially needed locations during other parts of the year.

A floating cemetery would allow for highlighted integration and placement of the deceased during times of remembrance without designating useable land for a single purpose. While still in the planning phase, the option of a movable cemetery opens many possibilities for the future in the name of accessible land scarcity in cities across the globe.

---

52 Cilento, Karen. "Columbarium at Sea / Tin-Shun But," *ArchDaily,* Accessed May 12, 2020.

HANGING CEMETERIES

GSAPP Lab at Columbia University in New York has proposed many potential architectural solutions and designs that address topics like land scarcity, environmental concerns, and usability with regard to future burial options in New York and other large cities.[53] One such idea proposed installing hanging luminescent pods under the bridges of New York City that would provide natural light powered by the energy produced by the decomposition process within. These pods would be alongside a memorial walk suspended beneath the city's current bridges.

Though this option stretches our comfort zone, and the way death and our daily lives interact, the suggestion does allow for dialogue and propels our culture as a whole toward an expanded idea of what a cemetery is and the way we interact with those who have passed away.

SOCIAL MOVEMENTS THAT ENABLE CONVERSATIONS ON THE END-OF-LIFE AND BEYOND

A number of communities address death and end of life in a community forum. Attending events hosted by groups in public settings or your home with friends can grow our understanding of the needs and wishes of those around us and help expand our knowledge on a subject that is often avoided.

---

53   "Death Lab," Columbia GSPP, Accessed June 1, 2020.

DEATH OVER DINNER

Death Over Dinner is a movement that offers guided conversation and insights that expand our knowledge on many topics that center around death. Resources can be found at deathoverdinner.org, which provides all the information and resources that you might need to have to host an event. According to the Death Over Dinner website, "It all started with a University of Washington graduate course called 'Let's Have Dinner and Talk About Death,' taught by Michael Hebb and Scott Macklin."[54] Since then, there have been more than one hundred thousand #deathdinners.

DEATH CAFES

According to deathcafe.com, "At a Death Café, people drink tea, eat cake, and discuss death. Our aim is to increase awareness of death to help people make the most of their (finite) lives." So far, more than ten thousand Death Cafés have been conducted based on a simple premise of conversations that never involve agendas, have set conclusions, or advertising. If you are interested in attending a Death Café, there may be one already meeting near you. If not, the website offers extensive resources to begin your own.[55]

DEATHPOSITIVE

In several major cities, DeathPositive groups meet to discuss very similar open discussions about death and end-of-life topics like DeathPositiveDC and DeathPositiveNYC that host

---

54   "Let's Have Dinner and Talk About Death," Death Over Dinner, Accessed May 12, 2020.

55   "What is Death Cafe," Death Cafe, Accessed June 1, 2020.

Death Cafés at local coffee shops and book club discussions based on end-of-life focused books.[56]

These events, like all those mentioned in this section, often have attendees who work in the hospice and funeral industry as well as body donation program workers, suicide prevention hotline volunteers, doctors, psychologists, death doulas, working professionals, and average Joes of all ages who sit down as equals with the hope to gain a deeper understanding of themselves and the world around them.

END-OF-LIFE ORIENTED CONFERENCES AND EVENTS

Reimagine, letsreimagine.org, is a group that designs city-wide conferences and events in San Francisco and New York City. According to their website, "Reimagine is a nonprofit sparking grassroots experiences and festivals that transform our approach to life and death."[57] With events ranging from guided meditations to expert panels and beyond, participants can explore life and death in a community and discover more about themselves and the world around them. Reimagining the way we look at the end of life brings new views and new ideas about ourselves.

In the end, having a conversation that allows us to become aware of the wishes of those around us on the subjects dealing with death and dying, allow us the opportunity to learn a lot about ourselves.

---

56   "About Death Positive DC," DeathPositiveDC, Accessed on May 12, 2020.
57   "What We Do." Reimagine. Accessed May 12, 2020.

CROWDSOURCED FUNERALS

In today's world of constant contact with multiple social networks, crowdsourcing has become a common path of raising funds for projects that range from making a movie to designing a new product to saving an endangered species.

Sites like GoFundMe.com and Kickstarter.com have made this mode of fundraising for a cause or project easier than ever. In other circumstances, campaigns have also been used to pay for someone's unexpected medical bills or help a single parent with a broken-down car. In many ways, it is a chance to pay it forward for the people who see and share the campaign to like and contribute what they can.

As part of a 2018 *New York Times* article, Laura Holson wrote, "GoFundMe, one of the largest fund-raising sites, says that 13 percent of its campaigns created in 2017 were described as memorials, which include funerals and are one of the company's fastest-growing categories…" Holson then quoted Rob Solomon, the chief executive of GoFundMe, who said, "'For many people, who have no other place to turn, we become the most important company to them.'"[58]

In instances when death comes at an unexpected time, in the prime of life or after a long and exhausting battle, finances for a funeral are not always readily available or set aside. In some instances, turning to the surrounding community is the only option that someone might have to pay for the funeral

---

58 Laura Holson, "As Funeral Crowdfunding Grows, So Do the Risks," *The New York Times*, June 5, 2018.ww

services of a loved one. Others may be able to cover the costs associated for the funeral but choose to turn toward a crowd-sourcing campaign to create scholarships, form memorials, or help the family pay down bills when life insurance was not yet a priority expense for a young family.

This growing trend has been made possible by the expansive reach of social networks in the modern world. Technologies advancing in this generation can create resources that have the potential to make hard times easier, but they also create scenarios for overspending. If a community raises funds for a young family that unexpectedly lost a parent, a reasonable goal should be set for funeral costs. As willing as some communities might be to fund a campaign for any monetary goal, not all of those funds need to be earmarked for overfunding a funeral just because the money is there. It is important to create an appropriate balance and remain inside reasonable means of spending, as is the case with many things in life.

When using an online crowdsourcing campaign, it is important to keep in mind that these funds are often not immediately available and have fees attached to what is raised. In most cases, funeral services require payment upfront. Meaning that the crowdsourcing campaign is in reality reimbursing a small bank loan, gap financing, or credit card that someone has used for payment. Since these funds were raised from external sources, they can be considered taxable income in some instances. Having some background knowledge does help when choosing how and where you choose to fund a funeral.

BUYER BEWARE

While many new options and opportunities are coming to light regarding funeral options, you have several things to consider.

Licensure and oversite provide a degree of protection to the consumer, and as many new options become available, it is important to choose a reputable source to help you make your selection. Be cautious of companies and individuals that want to offer help with your funeral that do not have legitimate training and education to do so. A facility that has a certified and licensed funeral director on staff who is not involved in events happening in the facility, while other "cheaper" or "less-trained staff" conduct all the actual tasks is a **red flag** of a business trying to skirt the law and something to avoid! If the only funeral director on staff is their off-site legal counsel, this is also something to avoid.

Confirm that the company and individuals working with your remains have the funeral licensure required from your State Funeral Licensing Board, since if they are not a licensed funeral director/funeral service provide/embalmer/mortician, this may be a warning sign! Some new options that are becoming available are attempting to sidestep professional and state oversight and should be closely monitored.

<u>Ask the big questions and look for proof that there will be follow-through.</u>

• What happens when this burial forest reaches capacity?

- What are the steps being taken to ensure that none of my composted remains are co-mingled with someone else's composted remains at any part of the process?

- Is a licensed funeral director always present in the facility and is working in that sole capacity? ("Oh, our 'XYZ' who isn't here is also our funeral director, don't worry it is totally legal," is not a good answer. "Oh, we aren't required to have a funeral director on staff," is another. If unsure, ask to see their license. If it is not posted in the establishment, that might be your chance to take a step back and ask around or make some calls.)

- What will happen in a hundred years when the roof needs to be replaced on this mausoleum? Will it be removed entirely? If the roof collapses, what is your course of action? Would I be responsible for repairs to my niche? (Some states require cemeteries to have perpetual care funds, to care for the grounds and facilities once the cemetery reaches capacity. Inquire about the future care plans of your burial location if this is a concern.)

Know that it is okay and encouraged to price shop and explore the possibilities that exist to you. Funeral homes are required by the Federal Trade Commission's "Funeral Rule" to give you a General Price List upon request along with other key documents.[59] While exploring your options in a time without a pressing need is always advisable, this is

---

59 "The FTC Funeral Rule," Federal Trade Commission, Accessed June 1, 2020.

not always possible and false urgency takes over. Take your time, do some research, and find what works for you.

Ask questions!

IT IS A LIFE LESSON

Realizing that many options are available, and that "what is perfect for one person, may not be perfect for the next," allows comfort in your decisions. Each option carries its own merit and offers a unique connection for the person it is used for, with no one choice being better than the other, just better for the individual. If someone says one option is better than another, they have not yet learned this valuable life lesson!

CHAPTER ELEVEN

VIRTUAL FUNERALS

Chime. "Hello, can you hear me? Is my mic on?"

"Yeah, we can hear you."

"Oh, hi. How are things up there?"

Chime. "Hello, is it working? I think they can see us. Can you see us?"

Virtual meetings have been evolving with the growth of technology. Technological growth has allowed us to hold conference calls live from every corner of the globe, host seminars for hundreds with breakout groups and shared materials, and to chat and have a happy hour with friends from whom we have been separated. The potential has existed for video conferencing technology to be adopted by numerous industries. Still, without a real pressing need, some may have been slower to adopt these new video technologies due to minimal demand.

Many funeral homes across the nation and world offered to broadcast services online, much like churches have provided, and post videos of services each week for individuals who were unable to attend in person. The equipment and concept were in place in most funeral homes. Still, the service in its entirety never wholly depended on the success of the streaming funeral in most cases, with nearly all those in attendance being physically present for the ceremony.

"It was something we offered but rarely used," a funeral director in Kansas shared. "For the most part, live streaming was a service that was only utilized in rare times when a single family member, maybe two, was unable to be present for one reason or another."

However, during the global Covid-19 pandemic in 2020, many industries, including the funeral industry, had to adapt quickly. With almost overnight restrictions involving social distancing limited most often to six feet, and the number of people allowed in a group often capped at ten people, a new normal required immediate change.

It was hard to imagine a scenario in which all funeral services would change in days, but that is what happened. Funeral homes switched to "by appointment only" arrangements, with heavy restrictions of personal protective equipment for the staff. As last responders came on the scene shortly after someone died of Covid-19, many unknowns had to be addressed.

In many scenarios, the immediate family of the deceased were the ones in self-quarantine, many of whom were suffering from the same symptoms. A shift to virtual services occurred faster than nearly any other change in the history of modern funerals. Those who were the most involved in the funeral or had the closest relationship to the deceased were now the ones unable to attend—making funerals at least for a time drastically different than they had ever been.

In an interview with Catherine Porter as part of "The Daily" podcast for the *New York Times,* Wayne Irwin, a retired minister at the United Church of Canada, was interviewed about his experience with virtual funeral services.[60] He had been helping the church go online after he retired, giving him a level in comfort and perspective with online services. Having done many funerals throughout his career, Irwin was able to pull on knowledge from differing periods of his life to create a virtual service for his wife Flora May that retained ritual and meaning for everyone able to participate. Irwin was able to create a service where the attendees were undistracted or encumbered with when to speak or what to sing.

The differences with the funeral were evident right from the beginning in the obituary. "So, when you see the bottom of her obit," Irwin pointed out, "it says an online celebration of life will take place on Saturday, April 11 at 10:30 a.m. at this website, with online visitation also available from 9:30. In lieu of flowers, please send donations here."

That is a significant change, especially for groups of people who may not know how to navigate video streaming sites, which makes planning key for an event like this.

---

60 Catherine Porter. "A New Way to Mourn." April 24, 2020 in The Daily, podcast, 46:35.

To prepare for the online service, Irwin started by saying, "*The service itself is a video.*" Irwin began by calling people and asking them if they could contribute something. From all over, extended family who probably would not make it to the funeral under normal circumstances were even able to take a more engaged role than during an in-person service. He called the ministers who would be involved. He called the organist, then the women who sang at their wedding, to help get others to sing along during the service. All of these individuals, except one of the ministers and the organist, would be attending from home.

As part of the service preparations, Irwin reached out to their grandchildren and asked for a small recording, roughly fifteen seconds, sharing a memory. These recordings could easily be recorded on Skype or cell phones then sent to the person packaging all the submissions together. With the knowledge that an hours-long service would be overly strenuous on most, brevity is always something to consider.

The short clips from grandchildren allow for longer recordings from children and spouses who would typically speak at the funeral service, giving them a bit more time and a chance to take a moment if needed or record a second take if it did not seem right. "Our daughter did a four-minute [video]," Irwin shared.

With all of these recordings from grandchildren, children, the organist, and singer and a few others, Irwin was able to stitch together a service that, on the day of broadcasting, participants would be able to view together from their homes over a Zoom call.

Numbering all the recordings and placing them in the correct order so that on the day of the service, the button could be pushed at the time of the service, and everyone could watch together was a big part of it. It meant everyone could join in the singing and as Irwin joked, "We can mute each other in case we're out of tune."

The words would roll down the screen as the organ played during the video. While many of those in attendance were singing along, you could even see a little girl dancing in one of the screens. An online service combines moments that you might see at a funeral and visitation together into a single display.

In the Zoom platform, the service took on a new aspect, not only could you see the service, but you could watch the other people in attendance. Some would be singing along, some crying, some showing smiles of joy while crying. In a way, the separation allows for people to open up in ways they would not in public, allowing in some cases for more outward emotion.

While many ways of conducting an online funeral ceremony exist, it seems helpful to put together a video or recordings that allow all involved to attend without tasks.

For a virtual service, plan ahead. Work closely with people who can design the service to your needs. Like a traditional service, family members work closely with the funeral home staff, ministers, and other services like clubs or veterans' groups. Having prerecorded messages that can be played as a video from different family members, friends, and groups, helps to create a service where everyone, including the family, can watch together. Having the words to songs played scrolling through the video allows everyone to take an active role and sing along to hymns or songs.

When hosting a virtual visitation, it can be helpful to make introductions and let people introduce themselves as they share a condolence or a memory. Having someone, whether the spouse or a close family member, be the "host" avoids most conversational hurtles. Having a virtual visitation also allows for participants to become familiar with the technology. Learning how to work the "mute" and "video" buttons and making smoother connections.

Does it feel like a funeral? In a way, it does. The funeral may not have the same familiarity as a physical funeral, but it fulfills one of the real purposes of a funeral, to come together and mourn the loss of a loved one. Virtual funerals are more inclusive in some ways and challenging in others. Feelings seem to rush over you even at such a great distance from each other. Tears of joy, sorrow, remembrance, and love seem to come from nowhere in the moment while everyone on a call is face to face. You can see others expressing a wide range of emotions with each face on the screen before you. Faces that might be unseen when physically present at a service. You are exposed but not, at the same time, in a way that creates closeness.

The adaption to change and shift to virtual technology and gatherings in an industry that seems unchanging comes with downsides, but with adaption and thought, technology has allowed us to be present for each other at deeply meaningful times in our lives. I would take that opportunity any day of the week.

CHAPTER TWELVE

HOW DID WE GET HERE?

___

Building Up to the Modern Funeral.

BURIAL

WHEN DID WE START BURYING OUR DEAD?

We have been dying for… well, logically, for almost as long as we have been living. Since the beginning of human life, humans have died, and for nearly as long, humans have been burying the dead. We have been burying our dead longer, in fact; the first undisputed evidence of an intentional burial was performed by our predecessors, the Neanderthals, during the Paleolithic Era roughly 130,000 years ago, at sites like Krapina in modern-day Croatia. The oldest known modern human burial that included rituals, on the other hand, was the burial of a presumed mother and child that took place at Qafzeh in Israel roughly one hundred thousand years ago.

What caused us to start burying our dead? That may be a question that is hard to answer and likely does not include a proven single decision that happened at a particular point in time. Paul Pettitt put it well in a paper on hominin evolutionary thanatology that "funerary rites are often about life. The living left behind after the death of a close one become 'social and psychological amputee(s).' Prolonged interaction with corpses may accelerate grieving processes, serving to reorganize society in the light of the deceased's altered relationship with it."[61] The way we process and find meaning in death on some level is a basic human need, and with the evolution of ritual and burial practices, we address this need.

According to the American Cemetery Association, the oldest continually maintained cemetery in the United States is the Miles Standish Burial Ground in Duxbury, Massachusetts, which placed a commemorative plaque on the cemetery grounds in 1977. Captain Miles Standish arrived on the *Mayflower* in 1620, and the cemetery was in use from 1638 until 1789. Oddly enough, I happen to have several family members buried in this pilgrim cemetery. The oldest intact carved gravestone in the cemetery is that of Captain Jonathan Alden, who died in 1697.[62] Jonathan was the son of *Mayflower* passengers John and Priscilla Mullins Alden, about whom Henry Wadsworth Longfellow wrote the endearing love story *The Courtship of Miles Standish* in 1858.

Today, societal preferences have led to cremation rates going higher than ever before. According to the Cremation

---

61 Paul Pettitt, "Hominin evolutionary thanatology from the mortuary to funerary realm: the palaeoanthropological bridge between chemistry and culture," Philosophical Transactions of the Royal Society B, Biological Sciences 373, no.1754 (July 2018).

62 Katherine H. Pillsbury, "*Duxbury, A Guide,*" Duxbury: Duxbury Rural and Historical Society (1999), 34.

Association of North America (CANA), in 2017, Nevada held the title for the highest percentage or cremations with an 80.1 percent cremation rate, while Mississippi had the lowest rate of cremations at 23.7 percent.[63] State-specific death statistics can be found by searching for the Vital Statistics information for your given state.

The increase in preference for cremation in North America has led to fewer traditional burials, while products like rental caskets have become widely used. These rental caskets have allowed families to have a traditional service without having to purchase an expensive casket for cremation. These caskets are equipped with rigid cardboard inserts that contain the decorative lining seen in a casket. After the services are held, the insert is rolled out of the casket shell through the foot end via an adapted hinge and locking door before a lid is attached to the rental casket insert, and it is ready for cremation. An outer container is required for cremation because this ensures that only one body can fit into the retort of a crematory at a time, eliminating any doubt on the matter.

What may seem to be an odd option to some, rental caskets are an option that many do not know about until they are informed about them. The importance of dialogue on the subject, and an ability to ask what feels like a strange or macabre question, might just be what it takes to establish a comfort level that promotes more helpful questions and solutions in the future.

---

63 "Industry Statistical Information," Cremation Association of North America (CANA), Accessed June 1, 2020.

I was once asked my opinion on taxidermy "since it is so similar to embalming." First, these are the kinds of questions that you receive and should encourage working in the funeral industry. Questions like this are often valuable learning moments and create the start of a dialogue and openness on the topic.

While embalming is the chemical treatment of the corpse using arterial injection, a process few people give any in-depth thought to on most days, taxidermy is not even close to a similar preparation of remains. Both embalming and taxidermy deal with death, but that is where similarities end.

Taxidermy, in most cases, is conducted by traditional skin-mount. Traditional skin mounting is a process that removes the skin of the deceased animal, leaving the internal organs untouched. A skilled taxidermist utilizing this method sees no blood or internal organs during the taxidermy. After the skin or hide is removed, it is treated or tanned before being placed on a rigid structure made of wood, wire, Styrofoam, or plastic that is the rough shape and size of the original animal. To be clear, making an incision much more significant than an inch without permission on human remains is technically considered desiccation of remains and is illegal. If taxidermy and embalming were similar, every embalmer in the country would be in prison so fast it would make your head spin.

The preparation of human remains requires extensive training. The art of embalming, as textbooks and course catalogs refer to it, is just that, an art form but also much more to the mind of an embalmer. The subtle details of chemicals with differing combinations needed on a case-by-case basis take real-world experience and textual knowledge to perfect.

These professionals learn techniques of preparation and how setting the features of the face can change the grieving process for the family. They have to develop extensive knowledge of anatomy, the circulatory system, and complicated cases because most people did not die without a real internal cause. If it was a blockage, that has to be worked around, or if an internal complication exists, adaptations have to be made. Perfecting abilities in the restorative arts is like practicing an art form. If you are missing an ear, the embalmer can make a replacement with hand-formed materials, then use their knowledge of makeup to blend in the artificial feature. Using cosmetics, they learn how to cut and style hair to match a picture provided by the family that might be twenty years old. The embalmer develops many diverse knowledge bases over an entire career, all for a singular role in the funeral home.

WHEN DID EMBALMING BECOME POPULAR?

Embalming in simple terms is the art and science of preservation designed to forestall decomposition, usually for public viewing, transportation, or medical preservation. While today the embalming process is done with chemicals, ancient culture developed embalming techniques and practices long before they became what they are today.

The ancient Egyptians used some of the earliest and most significant extents of preparation practices. Embalming and mummification practices go back as far as 3200 BC during the First Dynasty, but they were not alone. Embalming techniques can be found in antiquity from the Mayans and Aztecs cultures to the Meroites and Peruvians to Tibetan and Nigerian tribes.

Preservation techniques in Europe were quite rare until the time of the Roman Empire, with the first attempt to inject into the human vascular system recorded being attempted by Alessandra Gilliani before his death in 1326. With the Renaissance and the birth of modern medicine, many individuals such as Leonardo Da Vinci attempted and honed processes that led to the creation and techniques used in modern embalming.

The first to apply these new injection methods and knowledge of the arterial system into use for mortuary purposes was a Scottish surgeon, William Hunter, who wrote a widely read report on arterial and cavity embalming.

Methods that had previously been more widely used, like ice packing or laying the body on cooling boards, offered temporary delays of decay before services were held for family in neighboring towns before the adoption of embalming became more widespread.

Once the Civil War erupted, the citizens in the still-young United States of America still widely practiced home funerals and local burials. With small localized communities, it was easy to wash and dress a body for a funeral gathering in the family home without a need for embalming. With everyone who had the potential of attending living in relatively close vicinity of the deceased, time was less of a concern.

When the Civil War broke out, it was the first time in a still very young country in which communities had many friends and family dying far from home, which meant there were two options: bury the dead on the battlefield or in the town where they had fallen or find a way to combat decomposition to transport the deceased home from the battlefield for burial in their community. An outcry from communities to return their fallen soldiers home spoke volumes, and the rise of a technology and service called embalming became available to the masses.

In the depths of the Civil War, embalming broke away from the medical profession and began being practiced by undertakers. According to the National Museum of Civil War Medicine, "The embalming craze took off when an Army Medical Corps colonel (and close friend of President Lincoln) became the first Union officer to be killed. On May 24, 1861, Colonel Elmer Ellsworth was shot while removing a Confederate flag from the roof of a Virginian hotel... Thomas Holmes—later known as the "Father of Modern Embalming—offered his services to Ellsworth's family, and the captain's preserved body was taken to the White House, where it lay in state for several days. Afterward, he was taken to New York City, where thousands lined up to view the funeral cortege. Mourners on the route displayed a banner declaring, *Ellsworth, His blood cries for vengeance.*"[64] Following this occurrence, the Union and Confederate militaries authorized permits to private embalmers to work within military-controlled areas.

As the war came to a close, the final widespread connection point between the public and embalming came with the embalming of President Abraham Lincoln after his

---

64 "Embalming and the Civil War," National Museum of Civil War Medicine, Posted on February 20, 2016.

assassination in Ford's Theater. Lincoln's body, after embalming and public viewing, having laid-in-state on the same Lincoln Catafalque (a decorative casket stand) that is still used today in state funerals, was loaded onto a train to be taken home. Loaded onto the train with him was his son Willie, who had been embalmed and held in the Carroll family tomb in Oak Hill Cemetery in the nation's capital after dying of typhoid fever three years earlier. As planned, they were brought back to the tranquil rolling hills of their home in Springfield, Illinois after a funeral procession that traveled through stops in several cities for services along the journey.

WHEN DID FUNERALS START TO LOOK LIKE THEY DO TODAY?

After the Civil War, embalming began being widely used by the general public, which presented a need to train more embalmers. Thus, traveling mortuary schools like the Barnes School of Anatomy were born. These traveling schools began setting up shop in large cities to teach undertakers, as they were called at the time, the art of embalming. As more and more people trained in the art of embalming, the first seeds of the funeral profession were planted, springing to life funeral directing in the back of cabinetry shops, livery stables, and doctors' offices across the country.

Eventually, the needs of the undertaker who traveled to homes in the community outgrew their space in the backs of existing businesses like livery stables or carpentry shops, and they began establishing themselves as stand-alone businesses as the general public's preferences shifted to having funerals conducted in a separate home for funerals, which became funeral homes. They began to fill the need for a place outside of the family home at which the body could be prepared, and services could be conducted. Homes of funerals, funeral homes, funeral parlors, mortuaries, and many other similar business shingles were run by undertakers, morticians, funeral directors, and embalmers to serve the growing need for funeral services—a service that families could pay to conduct parts of the death and burial process they did not wish to do themselves.

While today most funeral services and preparations of a body are conducted inside a funeral home, there have always been opportunities for families to choose what works for them. Some families find comfort in performing preparation tasks like the washing of the body or service components like having a graveside burial service in a family cemetery on their farm.

One of the most significant misrepresentations of the funeral industry today is that you have to do everything at the funeral home. That is simply not true. The people at your local funeral home are there to provide services and help with your needs for funeral services and ceremonies. While a majority of funerals follow a similar format, with a bit of pre-planning to establish what is right for you, they can be there to help make the process easier.

Today funeral services are available in a myriad of different forms with differing cultural and religious orientations— from eco-friendly planning to traditional casketed burial, and any number of differing religions. Your funeral director is a resource to help you translate what you want into a realistic ceremony of remembrance, serving as a guide to discovering the way services in any given practice or religion have traditionally been conducted and answer the questions you might have about them. They also are there as a resource of information on how you might wish to alter and choose those ceremonies and services to fit your wants and beliefs.

While not all options are available in the span of a few days in some scenarios, with an organized and thought-out plan that is meaningful to you and your loved ones made in advance, options that you might not have known about or chosen before may become your reality.

CREMATION
Ashes to ashes, dust to dust...

It's something we all have a concept of or at least a saying we have heard, but when did we start using fire as a mode of final disposition? Did it begin with a funeral pyre on the banks of the Ganges in India? Was it perhaps a tradition learned from the Vikings catching on like wildfire with the release of a burning arrow aimed at a listing funerary boat?

Many possible sources could serve as the start of the integration of fire into funeral practices, as this practice spans the world over from every corner of the world, with some cultures sourcing their practice out of religious beliefs, and others out of practical necessity. Nearly every culture has used fire as part of funeral rituals at one point or another over time. While certain practices were widely used in a culture and point in time, perhaps being rooted in a legend that has fallen out of practical use, other practices evolved to suit the needs of our modern population.

One example of the creative integration of past practices and modern availability came in the form of a modern take on a Viking funeral. In a small lake community, the lake was as much a part of the community as anything else; one family thought a Viking funeral seemed like the perfect end for a lifelong resident. Since many complications arise when placing a deceased body on a boat in a lake and setting it ablaze, a creative solution was reached during the funeral planning process. It was decided that the intended goal of the Viking practice was for the complete cremation of the body before the boat sank to the bottom of the lake. So, traditional cremation was chosen as the mode of disposition, after which the ceremony could be conducted.

Standing on the edge of the lake surrounded by family and friends from the lake community, the ashes were placed on a model of a Viking longboat complete with oars and sail. Flammable material was added around the ashes with flowers, and a metal wire was attached to the sail as it was pushed out into the calm waters of the lake at sunset, with the sky glowing in the brilliant reds and oranges of a summer sunset.

As the funerary Viking boat slowed off the shore, a flaming ball attached to an eye hook slid down the thin metal cable toward the model boat before flame met the treated materials of the Viking sail, and the ship was set ablaze as dusk fell on the lake and the longboat vanished below the waves. This practice was a fitting modern recreation of an ancient practice in line with the wishes of the family.

Fire is seen in many ways by many cultures; it can be purifying, it can be healing, and it can be a fitting end for those who choose cremation as their preferred mode of disposition.

How we got to where we are now has a great deal to do with a single factor: us.

The needs we have had in our diverse and differing communities around the world have brought with them myriad ways of mourning and remembering those who have passed away. Services that have been provided by professionals, experts, shamans, religious leaders, holy societies, and elders throughout history have been just that, a service, which exists to aid those who cannot or do not want to perform them themselves. That is why how we got here and where we are going are a continuum of services designed to meet the needs of the communities we live in.

THE PINE BOX PARADOX

———

"Just put me in a simple pine box."

—MANY, MANY, MANY PEOPLE.

What if your idea of a pine box and the reality of what you are actually getting in terms of the goals of your funeral service are two different things?

To discover if your choice matches your preference, let's start by asking: What are you asking for by picking the pine box?

"Is a pine box even an option?"

The simple answer is: yes. Several forms have been designed to achieve the needs and justifications for the person selecting the plain pine box as an option. While it may not readily be on display as an option in some locations, if this is what you want, ask. But I would suggest reading the rest of this chapter before making your final decision to make sure you are getting exactly what you want.

"I want a plain pine box."

The first choice that is being made is in the name: pine. Pine is a fast and straight-growing tree that is widely available, while also being a soft wood, meaning it takes less working to create usable lumber. Being one of the most commercially and widely used types of lumber, pine maintains a relatively low cost in comparison to other types of wood, making pine a practical choice in availability and cost.

The second part of the name, box, is also worth discussing here. As the word describes, a plain pine box is often just that, a wooden rectangular box free of any extra shaping or decorative details. While pine casket would technically be correct, usually this implies a bit more design was used in the construction and esthetic. Calling it a box achieves a goal right off the bat, expressing a no-frills simplicity.

"I want a plain pine box because I like the way it looks."

If the look of the burial container is why you are choosing a plain pine box as your casket selection, it is precisely what you should get. People select caskets based on the preference of color, personality, ornamental feature, shape, design, overall look, and many other factors. What draws you to a final selection should be the traits that are important to YOU.

"I want the plain pine box because it is the best green option."

If you are selecting this as a **green alternative**, there may be more appealing options in existence that you might prefer.

"I want a green burial with a simple pine box as a casket." Then you may want to consider an Aron, a casket that contains no metal in their construction using instead wooden pegs and the use of joints to maintain the strength and rigidity of the casket. The Aron, as they are called, began being used in accordance with Jewish laws that require the casket to be made entirely of natural, biodegradable materials, which means using wood—no metal parts, with a plain, unlined interior. This option can be adapted if no religious or cultural limitations exist. The type of wood can vary—typically pine or redwood are used—but any acceptable wood with a plain or lightly polished exterior can be used. The minimal adornment of these caskets is usually thought of as a reminder of the equality of all people at death.

If this is the option you select, planning in advance may be wise for two reasons. First, the availability of this option might require ordering or making arrangements ahead of time because often they are made by hand by very few sources or suppliers. While some inventory is kept by these suppliers, they usually cannot expedite an order if inventory is low on a handmade item—not to mention the time needed for shipping if the person building it is on the other side of the country or does not use electronic communication. The second reason is dependent on whether you would like to be buried without an outer burial container surrounding the casket. These restrictions are important to consider because of cemetery rules about outer burial containers.

Many cemeteries require an outer burial container to prevent depressions from forming at the surface level of the cemetery once the casket has broken down over time. Cemeteries prefer level cemetery surfaces to make it easier to perform landscape maintenance and enable the use of machinery for burials in the surrounding burial plots in the future. If you would prefer not to use an outer burial container, find a cemetery that allows the pine box to be buried without a rigid outer burial vault made of concrete. In some cases, a six-piece box is what you will need to look for or clarify when pre-planning your funeral. A six-piece box is an outer burial container that is constructed from six pieces of concrete inside the grave at the time of burial.

Places to consider when looking for green burial options might include a family cemetery (an option only available in some parts of the country or with advance approval from a planning and zoning board), a green burial cemetery near you that allows a pine casket with no metal parts to be used, or some smaller country cemeteries.

Other creative options also exist if your goal is eco-responsibility. From woven basket burial containers to choices made of bamboo, new options are available constantly. One of the KEY FACTORS, if you would like to select an option that is outside the traditional options selected by the wider community is **PRE-PLAN FOR YOUR FUNERAL**.

Unique options can be made available when you need them on a timeline that suits the needs of your family and loved ones. It is horrible when a family comes in after a death occurs and finds out that the option they had had in mind has to be constructed on the other side of the country and will not be ready for weeks or months. As you can imagine, in most cases, this is a timeframe most families are not willing to entertain, which means they then have to select the closest option available to them at the time.

The casket you select does not affect your ability to have a public viewing. While some establishments might heavily suggest certain choices to be displayed at a public funeral, it is well within your rights to request an open casket with a plain pine box. Just because you are choosing an economically priced option with most plain pine boxes, it does not mean that you cannot have a traditional open casket at your funeral.

A quick aside about timing: unless bound by adherence to religious requirements, the funeral does not need to take place at a breakneck speed. Allow time between the death and services for people to travel into town and for your family to prepare. While having an open casket at a public viewing has some time limitations, with case-by-case scenarios affecting this timeline, there is usually more time than you think. If you are selecting cremation or having a private family burial and would like to receive friends at a later date, you may prefer an option for services at much later times. Personally, I have gained a great deal of closure seeing family members and friends one last time at their funeral, but what is right for one person or family may not be for the next. Considering these aspects is important when deciding what is right for you.

"I want it because it is the cheapest option!"

If low pricing is your intended goal in selecting a simple pine box, a better option for you probably exists. Often a pine box is a mid-price-point option. Cheaper options composed of corrugated cardboard with a veneer exterior have proven to be what someone had in mind in terms of the most economical choice.

Other options in other woods, or more expensive woods or precious metals with various levels of design and intricacy, exist for the same reason a plain pine box does. Remember that what is right for you might not be right for someone else. Where someone is in their life, what they have achieved, the way they see themselves or want to be seen can all play a part in their casket selection.

For every person who wears a Timex watch and drives a twenty-year-old pickup, someone else wears a Rolex and drives a brand-new Mercedes Benz, and yet another wears a Rolex and drives a twenty-year-old pickup. Having a wide variety of options allows you to make your funeral and the mental image people leave the services with uniquely yours. No one option is better than another. Just what is right for you and those you leave behind. If some else's choices differ from your selection, that is okay too.

"I want a pine box because I plan to build it myself."

If this is why you are selecting a plain pine box, numerous plans and designs are available for purchase online. It is crucial to be exact in these cases with the measurement of the outer measurements of the casket. While most caskets appear to be different, the exterior measurements are uniform unless it is an oversized casket. External measurements are an important detail if you would like to prevent extra costs in the future due to your casket being slightly too large to fit in the mausoleum or vault that you are using.

Another poignant point when considering building your casket is the strength of the end product. While many people undertake this endeavor sometime in advance of when they will die, they fail to consider any weight gain that might happen with age. Conversely, if the casket is constructed with too much reinforcement, it may become too heavy to be lifted by a team of six to eight pallbearers comfortably. In the end, it is important to do your research when constructing your casket. Opening a dialogue and planning in advance with your funeral home of choice and asking questions along the way will prove to be valuable resources.

The paradox of the pine box is one of selecting an option and having your justification for said choice align. Are you getting what you want or just following words that sounded good? The takeaway may be to look within yourself.

"*The boundaries which divide Life and Death*

are at best shadowy and vague.

Who shall say where the one ends,

and the other begins?"

—EDGAR ALLAN POE

CHAPTER THIRTEEN

DEATHITECTURE

———

Some of the most innovative and creative ideas when it comes
to funerals have come from the field of architecture. Cemetery architecture addresses how cemeteries and death, in
general, are integrated into our lives as an active and continued form of remembrance.

Most people visualize architecture with regard to the afterlife as a large monument. The pyramids and burial tombs of
ancient Egypt hold a place of fascination and wonder in our
minds, even millennia later. These monumental structures,
thought to be designed to be a site to prepare and secure safe
passage into the afterlife, integrated death into daily life in
a visual way. The catacombs of Paris combine massive engineering and construction in their seemingly endless maze
of passages with the needs of a modern and changing world
while remaining part of a bustling metropolis.

These monumental feats of architecture and engineering stand
out as common knowledge in the modern world. Simultaneously, other cultures have observed more temporary burial
markers, selecting materials that fade away and return to

nature as a way to remember the dead. Whether integrated into our communities or made into a special and separate space, where we choose to place and remember our dead is something that will not be lost to time. How we memorialize our dead will demonstrate to future cultures how the community we live in today interacts with those we have laid to rest.

Innovations in the way we create this space do not dismiss a past way of doing things as outdated or obsolete; rather, they provide new outlets for those who find comfort in a choice that is based in personal logic to a new and currently underserved community, those who do not fully connect with cemeteries in the modern world.

One of the most innovative groups working in this space is the Death Lab at Columbia University Graduate School of Architecture, Planning, and Preservation (GSAPP) in New York City.[65] The Death Lab's founder Karla Rothstein presents new ideas about what might be a future mode of disposition. Currently, the culture in the United States and in many countries around the world has a very rigid structure and image of what we envision when thinking about where bodies will be placed for eternity. That vision usually centers on a grave in a cemetery where someone will be buried and remain undisturbed forever.

This is not the case everywhere. In some parts of the world, the grave is rented for the period that the body decomposes, after which the remains are dug up and placed in an ossuary or crypt, making the grave usable for the next individual who needs it.

---

65   "Death Lab," Columbia GSPP, Accessed June 1, 2020.

The right to remain buried in the same grave forever in these places comes with a heavy price. The catacombs of Paris owe their existence to a time of high death rates due to sickness that outpaced the capacities of the cemeteries that existed in and around the city. Even though we think of a cemetery as being a rigid unchangeable idea, there have been many changes in how we bury people throughout recent history, from crypts that hold thousands of individuals' bones to ossuaries that contain the ashes of many. Some cemeteries were designed initially to be used as public parks in unison with the graves. The evolution of our cultural preferences has distanced us from many of these past practices. Practices that may very well fulfill the ecological or personalized goals we have for burials today.[66]

The "Light After Life" project centers around the fact that "bodies are rich sources of biomass—energy that can be converted in a manner that is both respectful to the living city and a fitting tribute of past individuality."[67] The proposed plan suggests a meandering walkway that could be infused into a cityscape, which holds within it a "constellation of serially reusable funerary vessels. that produce 'mourning light' that waxes and wanes during the organic conversion."[68]

The light derived from the biogas emitted as part of the controlled anaerobic bio-conversion that accelerates the decomposition of a corpse would allow for a small amount

---

66 Philippe Ariès, *The Hour of Our Death: The Classic History of Western Attitudes Toward Death Over the Last One Thousand Years.* Vintage; 2nd edition (July 22, 2008).
67 "Light After Life." Non Architecture Competitions. Accessed June 1, 2020.
68 "Light After Life."

of organic material to be returnable to the family after the decomposition process.

With options like human composting finding legalization in parts of the United States, options like Light after Life stand a chance of becoming an actual reality with public acceptance and integration.

Another of their proposed projects is called "Constellation Park" and takes the same bioluminescent decomposition vessels and integrates them in a stunning manifestation of a futurist cemetery suspended under the bridges of New York City. According to Death Lab, this project creates a suspended memorial space that could serve as a "collective urban cenotaph for intimate individual memorials."

The lifecycle of the illuminating vessels have more profound integrations with how we live utilizing a year-long cycle for the vessel. This year-long cycle draws on grief processes that coincide with the brightness and dimming of the lights that emit throughout the year. The brightest lights emerge in the first few months before they begin to grow dimmer throughout the year, ending with a release of the stored energy at the end of the roughly year-long process. The light then becomes bright again for the final few weeks.

As our world begins to consider our limited resources and space in densely populated urban landscapes, we might find benefit in forcing an evolution of thought. This evolution could bring the beauty of life and death back into our daily lives, whether by word, thought, or a light in the night sky.

CHAPTER FOURTEEN

THE LEGACY OF
A LIKENESS

———

"By the end of this year, there'll be nearly a billion peo-ple on this planet that actively use social networking sites. The one thing that all of them have in common is that they're going to die. While that might be a somewhat morbid thought, I think it has some really profound implications that are worth exploring."

—*ADAM OSTROW*[69]

The connections that we currently have to the people who have died are limited to very similar mediums that have remained constant through most of human existence. The immediate connection of the location of the human remains and the grave marker itself has been pervasive in cultures from ancient Egypt to the modern world today.

---

69 Adam Ostrow, "After Your Final Status Update," Filmed July 2011 at TEDGlobal 2011, video, 5:14

Next are all the remnants of that individual from throughout their life, from family photos and awards that held a place on a shelf, to a book they had written during their life (Hi, kids! [Dad, Grandpa, Great-Grandpa] Loves You!). Then there is everything else: the notes, the knick-knacks, and the memories, both tangible and intangible things that get passed down from generation to generation until the connection is lost or forgotten. Through the possibilities of innovation and technology, however, these connections we have to those who have died may be evolving more today than ever before.

A newly available option is writing a blog post in advance and setting it for publication after death, as a way to transition our life's work (our social media accounts and blogs) into an archive. These are perhaps the most in-depth and widespread archives of life ever to exist, documenting the likes and dislikes, highlights and sorrows, found throughout the lives of the famous and the not-so-famous the world over.

This is not a particularly new idea, as many prominent figures from the past scheduled a final work to be published at a predetermined interval after their death. Today more people than ever before have an audience on their social media accounts to receive their first posthumous post in context to all of their other posts and shares throughout their lives. Services like mykeeper.com, a collaborative online memorial platform to post and share memories, or ifidie.net let you create a message or video to be distributed after you die.

Currently, text predictors that use artificial intelligence (AI) like yes.thatcan.be/my/next/tweet/ can create a post of what you might potentially say or post based on analysis of past tweets. As this technology advances, might it be possible in the future for predictive conversational applications after a person has passed? If so, how will it be depicted? On a screen as part of an animated image, through the speakers of a programmable robot, or perhaps more lifelike than ever?

Holograms are another new way our digital selves could be used after we are gone. Examples of holograms being used in the entertainment industry exist even today.

As part of the *Michael Jackson: ONE* show, the lyrics of "The Man In The Mirror" seem fitting as a hologram of Michael Jackson takes the stage with live dancers in Las Vegas, giving an in-person connection for all those in attendance in a way that had not been possible to past generations after his death.

Legal considerations and hurdles limit the use of someone's image in some places. Several states already have laws that specifically address the usage of a personal likeness after they die, with authorization for use placed with the deceased's estate, who in turn have control over the commercial use of the dead person's likeness and image.[70]

California has laws that recognize rights to publicity and/or likeness post-death, while New York law notes those rights end upon death. These laws are changing quickly and often are very different in state or local ordinances. When speaking with a lawyer about your will and planning for the future of

---

70 Robinson, Cori. "Death and The Holograms: Celebrities Continue To Generate Revenue And Problems After Death. " *Above The Law*. November 6, 2018.

your estate, the rights to your likeness after your death would be a good question to raise if they concern you.

Tupac Shakur was also able to take the stage during Coachella using a hologram-like technique used in the theater called Pepper's Ghost, which utilized a two-dimensional projection onto angled glass to create a life-like performance. Tupac's presence on stage, however, took some logistical and legal work. Dr. Dre and his production team, alongside Tupac's estate, had to handle the ramifications of using Tupac's likeness, requiring the approval and blessing of his mother, Afeni Shakura.[71]

> *"For every dark night, there's a brighter day."*
>
> —TUPAC SHAKUR

Even when legal rights are given, the ethical concerns of using someone's image after they have died remain. The ethics behind the use of holograms, like many other new technologies, are still developing as they come into broader usage.

It may be beneficial to clarify your wishes for the use of your image and likeness after your death to the person you designated to be in charge of your estate once you are gone. Making your wishes clear at the very least eliminates any doubt about your opinion on the subject for those you leave behind.

---

71 Dodson, Aaron. "'The strange legacy of Tupac's 'hologram' lives on five years after its historic Coachella debut." *The Undefeated.* April 14, 2017.

We should keep in mind that, in a way, this is a continuation of music, books, and movies we see every day. Long after death, musicians stay alive through their music, which is played on radio stations and in our homes with rights and royalties that are still actively paid to estates. Movie stars stay alive by way of streaming films, television, and advertisements across the globe with similar perpetual use. Authors stay alive in their words or audiobook readings of their work.

Closer to home, friends and family stay alive in voicemails, texts, and notes left behind. Moments as simple as finding hair in the brush of a deceased loved one can incite emotion, just as emotions can be triggered by things you leave behind.

With technological advances, the way we communicate with the dead may not be bound to the photographs and work that someone has done during their lives for much longer. These new and cutting-edge changes in the way we interact, however, mean that the current generation will have to make choices that have never had to be made before.

A few questions in this area worth thinking about might help develop what you are comfortable with regarding the future use of your likeness.

DO I WANT TO BE A HOLOGRAM AFTER I'M GONE?

In some settings, just as a picture or video might be comforting to those we leave behind, it is worth considering that a hologram might have a place in the way we are remembered in the future. While some technologies integrate predictive speech to enable conversations, others rely on prerecorded messages, akin to the famed message from Princess Leia Organa that R2-D2 shares, showing her pleading for Obi-Wan Kenobi's help in *Stars Wars Episode VI: A New Hope*, directed by George Lucas in 1977. A prerecorded message may be of some comfort to some families, while others might be unsettled. The medium in which a remembrance is made available should be chosen based on you and those you leave behind.

Computer programs already exist that can reproduce someone's likeness superimposed over another to make a photo or video look as if anyone is actually partaking in the scene; these so-called "Deepfake" videos have already become controversial and are banned from a number of sites, but the fact that they exist only lends to the future possibilities of whether our likeness could be used in similar software.

SHOULD ANYONE BE ABLE TO ACCESS MY SOCIAL MEDIA POSTS AFTER I'M GONE?

Who has access to your social media posts once you are gone is a choice that is specific to you. If you do have strong feelings one way or another, it is essential to record this somewhere that is accessible to the person carrying out your wishes after you are gone. It might be beneficial to have a conversation with those you leave behind to gauge the importance of the material and how it might be helpful to each of them. In some scenarios, a photo that is accessible anywhere anytime with a simple search may be comforting. In other settings, limiting exposure might be the preferred course of action depending on your and your family's comfort level.

WHO HAS THE RIGHTS TO MY HOLOGRAM, SOCIAL MEDIA, ETC.?

In many states, the person or persons who are left in control of your estate would be in charge of the perpetual care and use of your image or likeness—making your wishes known to these individuals like many other financial and medical decisions can eliminate future doubts and ethical questions that arise. It could also depend on local laws—it makes sense to write down what you want and talk to the person you designate to be the steward of your digital remains. A great tool to start this journey is the Digital Remains Planning Guide found at the end of this book. Planning out your wishes for your online presence and the future of your likeness helps alleviate the future burden of family members in the event that a decision is needed. Completing the simple guide and discussing it with your Designated Digital Remains Steward can ensure that even though laws are constantly evolving in this area, your wishes are carried out to the best of their abilities.

WHAT IF I POSTHUMOUSLY WENT VIRAL?

From authors to singers, works that are released posthumously have delivered a mixed bag of results. Some wait to release a sequel until after their death, while others fear that the work will be misrepresented through a filter of sentimentality. In the end, if the thought of something you did during your life becoming wildly popular provokes a feeling, analyze what makes you feel that way and plan a path that is right for you.

FINDING THE BALANCE IN CHANGING TIMES

In an age of new technologies, we have to prepare for a new and changing world. With a changing world comes the benefits that come with change. Social media has opened the world up to new communities and with it comes online archives of our lives. As we come to the end of our lives and plan for our financial retirement, finalize wills and estates, and select the funeral options that are right for each of us, so too do we need to plan for the future of our digital remains. How we adapt and learn from lessons like that of Chris and his experience with shocking news on social media or the wisdom we learned from Lux's analysis of the *New York Times* Editorial Obituaries, can factor greatly into making the future better for ourselves and our fellow man when we deal with death.

"To the well-organized mind,

death is but the next great adventure."

—J.K. ROWLING

THE SOCIAL MEDIA CLEAN-UP GUIDE

———

Now that we have highlighted a number of thoughts and ideas around social media and what they mean, let's explore just how to make our wishes for our digital remains a reality. While we cannot predict the future, we can at least prepare for it. While we still have the ability to make decisions for ourselves, social media should be a main area of concern for the tech generation in planning for the future.

Considering the high value we often place on widely shared photographs and videos of ourselves and those around us, like those found on our Instagram feed and other social media sites, it is essential to consider all platforms when planning for digital eternity.

What one can do to prepare for death when it comes to your or a loved one's social media accounts? And what should be done with someone's social media accounts after they are gone?

SOCIAL MEDIA BY THE NUMBERS

It helps to have an idea of just how many accounts over the next one hundred years will have to be either deleted, memorialized, or left unchanged per the respective company's policies on the maintenance of accounts, profiles, and channels after someone passes away. As of 2020, the number of social media users is already sky-high and will only expand with the inflation of global populations and additional access becomes more readily available.

Number of Users as of 2020[72]

Facebook: 2,414,000,000

Instagram: 1,000,000,000

WhatsApp: 1,600,000,000

Facebook Messenger: 1,300,000,000

YouTube: 2,000,000,000

WeChat: 1,133,000,000

QQ: 808,000,000

QZone: 554,000,000

Douyin/TikTok: 500,000,000

Sina Weibo: 486,000,000

Reddit: 330,000,000

Snapchat: 314,000,000

Twitter: 330,000,000

LinkedIn: 310,000,000

Pinterest: 300,000,000

Many policies about death and memorialization are similar among the major social media sites. Highlighting the

---

72 "Most popular social networks worldwide as of April 2020, ranked by number of active users," Social Media and User-Generated Content, Statista, Accessed June 1, 2020.

platforms with the most users and the variations in policies and procedures required after a person has died can help us develop a better understanding of what information is necessary. Studying these policies will also help us grasp how the process works and who to consider before the end comes when planning what should happen with our social media accounts.

If you are trying to find information on how a particular social media site handles account status following the death of a user, as well as who and what kind of access a direct family member might have, direct your search to the Contact Us link on the desired website. From there, search for "Death of a User" or reach out to the company directly through their Help section.

FACEBOOK
For an in-depth look at how to convert your Facebook page to a memorial page or delete a Facebook account entirely, please refer to the *Digital Remains* chapter of this book.

INSTAGRAM
Instagram currently maintains a notification policy where if a direct family member notifies them of the death of the account holder, the account can be deleted or memorialized following some email correspondence with the company that includes information confirming the death, such as an obituary or news article. The deceased's account then has a "remembering" banner added to the heading on their page. The account and photos housed on a "remembering" page will not be deleted, but once the remembrance conversation

happens, the account will no longer appear in search results. If no one contacts Instagram, the account remains active and available to be viewed by those who are allowed to see past posts according to the privacy settings.

In regards to viewability of an account that is memorialized on their platform, Instagram says, "We try to prevent references to memorialized accounts from appearing on Instagram in ways that may be upsetting to the person's friends and family, and we also take measures to protect the privacy of the deceased person by securing the account."[73]

Planning for what is done with your Instagram account following your death might involve sharing where to find usernames and passwords in a secure location. Sharing this information might be the preferred course of action if you wish for someone to have access to your account after you are gone.

Instagram will not grant access to the account to anyone regardless of the circumstances, including death, stating, "It's always against our policies for someone to log into another person's account."

Often the photographs on Instagram feature a person in a form they felt inclined to share with others and showcases some of the highlights that occurred throughout their life. Whether these photos are maintained on Instagram or backed up on someone's phone, cloud, or computer, they can be significant to circles of friends and family. I, for one,

---

73 How do I report a deceased person's account on Instagram?" Help Center, Privacy and Safety Center, Instagram, Accessed June 1, 2020.

would highly recommend finding a way to save the photos shared on an Instagram account in a way that is accessible at a later date for friends and family.

Without a plan in place ahead of time, it becomes uncertain what path a direct family member will choose for your Instagram account and if that is in line with your wishes for your digital remains. It is not only important to consider what you would like done with these posts but whether your family might find comfort in utilizing these photos as a medium of remembrance.

TWITTER

Twitter provides a straightforward approach for the transition of an account after a person passes away.

Twitter's policies state, "In the event of the death of a Twitter user, we can work with a person authorized to act on behalf of the estate, or with a verified immediate family member of the deceased to have an account deactivated."[74]

After this request, Twitter will follow up with the notifying person for more information that might range from the notifier's identification confirmation to a copy of the deceased's death certificate. While the latter does sound burdensome at first, confirming that an account should be altered is a critical privacy matter. After Twitter confirms, the account is deleted. Twitter is, however, unable to provide account

---

74   "How to contact Twitter about a deceased family member's account," Rules and Policies, Twitter, Accessed on May 28, 2020.

access to the account itself, sharing, "We are unable to provide account access to anyone regardless of their relationship to the deceased."

Pre-planning for your digital remains is an important step in establishing what is, and is not, online after your death. With a plan that is known to someone who will be able to share your wishes for information on various social media accounts, it becomes possible to align your wishes for your accounts post mortem with reality.

SNAPCHAT

Snapchat allows for the deletion of an account if a person passes away. Following the Contact Us link you can select, "The person passed away" from the options, which then brings up the following message:

We are so sorry for your loss. We would like to assist you in any way possible.

Our privacy policies do not allow us to grant access to the account.

We can delete the account for you if you provide us with a copy of the death certificate.[75]

With some additional contact information from the notifier like name and email address, your account can be deleted.

---

75   "Snapchat Support," Contact Us, Snapchat, Accessed June 1, 2020.

Like other social media, account access is not permitted regardless of circumstances.

Once Snapchat has been notified, the account is placed in a deactivated status for thirty days, after which it will be permanently deleted. Within the thirty days, the account is recoverable if someone logs into the account.

If you would like your Snapchat account deleted after your death, you should make these plans before needing them. Designate a close friend or family member who will be actively involved in your funeral planning to deactivate your account.

TIKTOK

TikTok is a social media platform designed to be a "leading destination for short-form mobile video... [whose] mission is to inspire creativity and bring joy."[76] Some social media platforms are designed to give access to shared posts that maintain unless individually deleted even after an account is deleted. In new platforms, the only way to remove the account of a user after a death is to directly contact the company, as is the case with TikTok if you do not have the proper username and password information to log in.

POST AT YOUR OWN RISK

While many new social media have a learning curve regarding the death of a user as they grow, in rare cases, they are

---

76   "Contact," Tiktok, Accessed June 1, 2020.

ingrained in death itself. Multiple online trackers exist that tally deaths in relation to social media like TikTok. In some extreme circumstances, the attempted stunts performed for a post lead to deadly outcomes. Some examples of headlines are:

Sialkot boy loses life as pistol goes off while filming TikTok video with friends[77]

Four youths fell into the river. Three of them recovered but one died while making TikTok video[78]

Remember that a post is never worth your life.

YOUTUBE

To close the account of a deceased user's channel on You-Tube, you will need to visit YouTube's parent company's page, support.google.com, and then search for "close a deceased user's account." From there, you can select the desired action to close the account or request data by filling out the form provided.

PINTEREST

A Pinterest account can be deleted following a person's death by sending an email to care@pinterest.com. Anyone can send an email informing the company of the death of a user, opening up this task to a broader group of individuals.

---

77 Hussaini, Syed Umarullah. "Sialkot Boy Loses Life Taping Tik Tok Video," *BOL News,* December 29, 2019.

78 Das, Mesheeka. "TikTok again took a young man's life, fell into the river but still no clue was found," *News Track Live,* September 30, 2019.

In the email, include the name and email address of the deceased, as well as a link to their Pinterest page (this will start with www.pinterest.com). Additionally, you will need to include proof of death—an obituary or scanned copy of the death certificate—and proof of your connection to the deceased (i.e., a family tree, your name in the obituary, a marriage certificate, etc.).[79]

LINKEDIN

LinkedIn allows a broader field of individuals to make the initial report of a death, allowing friends or business connections to reach out to the company. While the amount of information that sites require can seem like a burden, LinkedIn reminds those reporting the death of a user, "We'll use this information to make sure we're removing the correct profile."[80] This step is essential, as it requires checks and double-checks to avoid a false report or the removal of the wrong account.

In the Contact Us section, you can select the "Request removal of a deceased member's LinkedIn profile" form from the available options. The form can be filled out by anyone but does ask for your connection to the deceased, allowing for the selection of Immediate Family, Extended Family, Non-Family, or Other. The form requests the notifier's information as well as the information of the deceased person, including the link to their LinkedIn account and obituary information if available.

---

79 "Privacy Policy," Pinterest, Accessed June 1, 2020.
80 "Request removal of a deceased member's LinkedIn profile," Contact Us, LinkedIn, Accessed June 1, 2020.

LAST WORD

While it is important to mention that the policies and procedures that center around what can be done with a user's account after they have died are continuously changing, and new social media outlets popping up more frequently, they hopefully are evolving toward a better means of memorializing those who pass away.

These social media companies have a growing role as the archivists and outlets for friends and family to memorialize those who have passed away. With this responsibility comes the need to allow users to plan what is done with their digital remains following their death.

If posting the status of the death of a family member via social media becomes too stressful, or managing the account settings of the deceased becomes overwhelming, remember that you have time to make these changes. While it is important to make these changes in a timely fashion to successfully adhere to the deceased's wishes, you do have time.

Taking the opportunity to make these reports and changes at a pace that works for you is important. Set a goal to start with the social media sites that you use to distribute service information to friends. These are the most time-sensitive posts since the faster the information becomes available, the more friends and family are able to see it. From there, write out a list of other social media sites potentially used and check off one or two at a time over a week.

IMPORTANT:

When sharing service information over social media, make sure that the service times have been finalized before sharing. Often initial planning times are still subject to change due to restrictions with schedules at churches, cemeteries, and funeral homes, as well as religious leaders' schedules and many other variables. A good point at which to share service information is after a formal obituary has been written and is sent to the paper or posted on an obituary website, like those found on funeral home websites.

If you are planning the services without assistance from a funeral director, it is a good idea to write out a short obituary that includes service information with family and close acquaintances who are in charge of the planning process. This obituary allows everyone to leave with the same agreed-upon details and times. After all, additional stresses from miscommunication can make a hard time even harder.

Four Steps to Take:

1. Make a list of your social media accounts.
2. Develop a plan for each of your social media accounts, designating which you would like deleted and which you would like memorialized.
3. Designate a person to be in charge of sharing funeral service information and your obituary as well as reaching out to social media sites for conversion to memorial accounts after you are gone. It is advisable to have this person be someone in your immediate family or someone

who can prove a close, direct relationship with you who each website will accept.

4. Share your plans for your digital remains (all the information available online about you) with your Designated Digital Remains Steward and confirm they are willing and able to reach out to the sites laid out in your plan. It is also advisable to talk through these plans and to weigh the desires of those remembering you when deciding your final arrangements.

DIGITAL REMAINS
PLANNING GUIDE

———

Planning for anything that concerns the end of life can be a difficult hurdle for many of us. These plans can be stressful and take time for you to carry out successfully, but they are a great help to your future self and your family.

These plans can include:
- Selecting Medicaid and Medicare options
- Claiming Social Security
- Completing an Advanced Care Directive
- Making a Last Will and Testament
- Selecting, planning, and funding your funeral plans
- And many other personalized documents and choices.

With the large amount of personal data we now have online, we now should include a plan for our digital remains to be placed alongside other important documents to advise those we leave behind how we want this archive of data to be treated after our deaths.

Each member of your household would benefit from completing the following Digital Remains Planning Guide and choosing a Designated Digital Remains Steward. The guide can be removed from this book and copied for best results; otherwise, gift your family members a copy of *Digital Remains* to have as their own. (I know the author would appreciate it.)

When selecting a Designated Digital Remains Steward, it is advisable to select a single close family member to carry out your wishes for your digital remains. Choosing a family member eliminates some requirements for an immediate family member to confirm death for some websites, but if the circumstances do not allow for this, you can select someone you trust to carry out your wishes. If you select someone outside of your immediate family, they may need access to a copy of your death certificate, so it is advisable to make a note that a copy is needed for this in your funeral plans.

The chapter entitled *The Social Media Clean Up Guide* in this book can serve as a great site-by-site guide for your Designated Digital Remains Steward, as it answers questions about where to go and how to carry out your wishes for your digital remains.

Social media will change in the future. How to carry out these preferences may also change as social media websites grow and adapt to new technologies and innovations. This guide helps set a tone for your wishes to be carried out most successfully.

Finally, this is not and does not constitute legal advice or recommendations. You should not rely on this chapter as anything other than a guide to express your preferences. If you have questions you should consult with an attorney.

DIGITAL REMAINS
PLAN FOR

———

_____

(YOUR FULL NAME)

Date: _____

**THE FOLLOWING IS A LIST OF
HOW I WISH FOR MY ONLINE PRESENCE
— MY DIGITAL REMAINS —
TO BE HANDLED AFTER I DIE.**

*Fill in blanks with your personal information
and check the boxes that apply to you.*

EMAIL

Account 1) _____ _____

(johndoe@email.com)

Password can be found: _____

☐ I wish for all emails and archives as well as my email address to be DELETED in their entirety to furthest extent possible.

☐ I would like all of my emails and email archives to be SAVED in a convenient medium for the potential future use of my heirs.

☐ I would like NOTHING DONE with my email after I am gone.

☐ No Preference

Account 2) _____ _____

(johndoe@email.com)

Password can be found: _____

☐ I wish for all emails and archives as well as my email address to be DELETED in entirety to furthest extent possible.

☐ I would like all of my emails and email archives to be SAVED in a convenient medium for the potential future use of my heirs.

☐ I would like NOTHING DONE with my email after I am gone.

☐ No Preference

Account 3) _____
(johndoe@email.com)

Password can be found: _____

☐ I wish for all emails and archives as well as my email address to be DELETED in entirety to furthest extent possible.

☐ I would like all of my emails and email archives to be SAVED in a convenient medium for the potential future use of my heirs.

☐ I would like NOTHING DONE with my email after I am gone.

☐ No Preference

Initial _____

SOCIAL MEDIA

FACEBOOK

My Username is: _____

My Password can be found: _____

☐ Convert my Facebook account to A MEMORIAL PAGE. (This option adds 'Remembering' to your account and removes your account from search results.)

☐ My Facebook Account
- I designate _____ to convert my page.

- I have chosen to:
  - ☐ DELETE my Facebook Account
  - ☐ Convert my Facebook to a Memorial Account
  - ☐ I designated this on Facebook.
  - ☐ I have expressed my wishes to this person.
☐ No Preference

Initial _____

TWITTER

My Username is: _____

My Password can be found: _____

☐ DO NOTHING to my TWITTER account.
☐ DELETE my Twitter Account
☐ No Preference

Initial _____

INSTAGRAM

My Username is: _____

My Password can be found: _____

☐ Convert my Instagram account to A MEMORIAL PAGE.
(This option adds 'Remembering' to your account and removes your account from search results.)

☐ DELETE my Instagram Account
- I designate _____ to convert my page.
  - ☐ I designated this on Instagram.
  - ☐ I have expressed my wishes to this person.
  - ☐ No Preference

Initial _____

SNAPCHAT

My Username is: _____

My Password can be found: _____

☐ Notify Snapchat of my death.
☐ No Preference

Initial _____

OTHER: _____

My Username is: _____

My Password can be found: _____
☐ Convert my _____ account to A MEMORIAL PAGE.
☐ DELETE my _____ Account.
- I designate_____ to convert my page.
  - ☐ I designated this on _____.
  - ☐ I have expressed my wishes to this person.

Initial _____

FUTURE APPLICATIONS OF MY ONLINE DATA/PRESENCE:

HOLOGRAM:

☐ I grant my heirs the UNLIMITED rights in perpetuity to the use of my likeness in any holographic or similar media in existence or yet-to-be-determined media.

☐ I grant my heirs the LIMITED rights in perpetuity to the use of my likeness in any holographic or similar media in existence or yet-to-be-determined media.

• Please adhere to the following stipulations regarding my holographic image to the best of your abilities:

_____

_____

_____

☐ No Preference; the use of my likeness for holographic use is the right of my heirs.

Initial _____

PREDICTIVE TEXT SOFTWARE:

☐ I grant my heirs the UNLIMITED rights in perpetuity to the use of my likeness in any Predictive Text Software or similar media in existence or yet-to-be-determined media to answer questions as I would, based on information that exists as part of my online presence including but not limited to Facebook, Instagram, Twitter, email, blogs, etc.

☐ I grant my heirs the LIMITED rights in perpetuity to the use of my likeness in any Predictive Text Software or similar media in existence or yet-to-be-determined media to answer questions as I would, based on information that exists as part of my online presence including but not limited to Facebook, Instagram, Twitter, email, blogs, etc.

- Please adhere to the following stipulations regarding my holographic image to the best of your abilities:

_____

_____

_____

_____

☐ No Preference; the use of my likeness for holographic use is the right of my heirs.

Initial _____

FUTURE DIGITAL PROPRIETARY USE OF MY LIKENESS:

☐ My heirs may have UNLIMITED use of my likeness for proprietary and commercial use after my death.

☐ I wish for the use of my likeness to be LIMITED to those uses allowed before my death.

☐ DO NOT use my likeness for proprietary or commercial reasons after my death.

Initial _____

I have left some final thoughts/final words/obituary ideas etc. in the following locations (memorial websites, blogs, physical location):

_____

_____

_____

_____

Explanation/Justification of my wishes for my online presence once I have passed away:

_____

_____

_____

_____

I have designated _____ (Name of Designee) as my Designated Digital Remains Steward to act as the person to carry out my wishes for my Digital Remains.

Date: _____   Signature:

_____

DIGITAL REMAINS
PLAN FOR

———

_____

(YOUR FULL NAME)

FOR RETENTION OF MY DESIGNATED DIGITAL
REMAINS STEWARD

_____

(Designated Digital Remains Steward's Name)

This is a duplicate letter to be given to my <u>Designated Digital Remains Steward</u> who I wish to be responsible for carrying out my wishes for my online presence to the best of their abilities, with the stipulation that technological changes in the future may promote or impede their ability to carry out these wishes and preferences in absolution in some instances.

☐ I understand that my Designated Digital Remains Steward needs to be someone in my immediate family; otherwise, this person will need access to proof of my death (i.e. my death certificate) and it may take some time for my wishes to be carried out after my death in some instances.

Dear _____,

In the event of my death, I would like you to carry out the following plans for my DIGITAL REMAINS (my online presence that exists after my death). A copy of the following wishes has been placed with my Will and other important legal paperwork unless otherwise noted. Further information on the subject of digital remains can be found in the book: *Digital Remains: Death, Dying, and Remembrance in the Tech Generation* by J.H. Harrington.

The Social Media Clean Up Guide in *Digital Remains* can serve as a great site-by-site guide for you, the Designated Digital Remains Steward. It instructs you where to go and how to carry out the following wishes for my Digital Remains.

Date: _____

**THE FOLLOWING IS A LIST OF
HOW I WISH FOR MY ONLINE PRESENCE
— MY DIGITAL REMAINS —
TO BE HANDLED AFTER I HAVE DIED.**

*Fill in blanks with your personal information
and check the boxes that apply to you.*

EMAIL

Account 1) _____

(johndoe@email.com)

Password can be found: _____

- ☐ I wish for all emails and archives as well as my email address to be DELETED in their entirety to furthest extent possible.
- ☐ I would like all of my emails and email archives to be SAVED in a convenient medium for the potential future use of my heirs.
- ☐ I would like NOTHING DONE with my email after I am gone.
- ☐ No Preference

Account 2) _____

(johndoe@email.com)

Password can be found: _____

- ☐ I wish for all emails and archives as well as my email address to be DELETED in entirety to furthest extent possible.
- ☐ I would like all of my emails and email archives to be SAVED in a convenient medium for the potential future use of my heirs.
- ☐ I would like NOTHING DONE with my email after I am gone.
- ☐ No Preference

Account 3) _____
(johndoe@email.com)

Password can be found: _____

☐ I wish for all emails and archives as well as my email address to be DELETED in entirety to furthest extent possible.
☐ I would like all of my emails and email archives to be SAVED in a convenient medium for the potential future use of my heirs.
☐ I would like NOTHING DONE with my email after I am gone.
☐ No Preference

Initial _____

SOCIAL MEDIA

FACEBOOK

My Username is: _____

My Password can be found: _____

☐ Convert my Facebook account to A MEMORIAL PAGE. (This option adds 'Remembering' to your account and removes your account from search results.)
☐ My Facebook Account
• I designate _____
to convert my page.

- I have chosen to:
  - ☐ DELETE my Facebook Account
  - ☐ Convert my Facebook to a Memorial Account
  - ☐ I designated this on Facebook.
  - ☐ I have expressed my wishes to this person.
☐ No Preference

Initial _____

TWITTER

My Username is: _____

My Password can be found: _____

☐ DO NOTHING to my TWITTER account.
☐ DELETE my Twitter Account
☐ No Preference

Initial _____

INSTAGRAM

My Username is: _____

My Password can be found: _____

☐ Convert my Instagram account to A MEMORIAL PAGE. (This option adds 'Remembering' to your account and removes your account from search results.)

☐ DELETE my Instagram Account
- I designate _____ to convert my page.
  - ☐ I designated this on Instagram.
  - ☐ I have expressed my wishes to this person.
  - ☐ No Preference

Initial _____

SNAPCHAT

My Username is: _____

My Password can be found: _____

☐ Notify Snapchat of my death.
☐ No Preference

Initial _____

OTHER: _____

My Username is: _____

My Password can be found: _____

☐ Convert my _____ account to A MEMORIAL PAGE.
☐ DELETE my _____ Account.
- I designate_____ to convert my page.
  - ☐ I designated this on _____.
  - ☐ I have expressed my wishes to this person.

Initial _____

FUTURE APPLICATIONS OF MY ONLINE DATA/PRESENCE:

HOLOGRAM:

☐ I grant my heirs the UNLIMITED rights in perpetuity to the use of my likeness in any holographic or similar media in existence or yet-to-be-determined media.

☐ I grant my heirs the LIMITED rights in perpetuity to the use of my likeness in any holographic or similar media in existence or yet-to-be-determined media.

- Please adhere to the following stipulations regarding my holographic image to the best of your abilities:

_____

_____

_____

☐ No Preference; the use of my likeness for holographic use is the right of my heirs.

Initial _____

PREDICTIVE TEXT SOFTWARE:

☐ I grant my heirs the UNLIMITED rights in perpetuity to the use of my likeness in any Predictive Text Software or similar media in existence or yet-to-be-determined media to answer questions as I would, based on information that exists as part of my online presence including but not limited to Facebook, Instagram, Twitter, email, blogs, etc.

☐ I grant my heirs the LIMITED rights in perpetuity to the use of my likeness in any Predictive Text Software or similar media in existence or yet-to-be-determined media to answer questions as I would, based on information that exists as part of my online presence including but not limited to Facebook, Instagram, Twitter, email, blogs, etc.

- Please adhere to the following stipulations regarding my holographic image to the best of your abilities:

_____

_____

_____

_____

☐ No Preference; the use of my likeness for holographic use is the right of my heirs.

Initial _____

FUTURE DIGITAL PROPRIETARY USE OF MY LIKENESS:

☐ My heirs may have UNLIMITED use of my likeness for proprietary and commercial use after my death.

☐ I wish for the use of my likeness to be LIMITED to those uses allowed before my death.

☐ DO NOT use my likeness for proprietary or commercial reasons after my death.

Initial _____

I have left some final thoughts/final words/obituary ideas etc. in the following locations (memorial websites, blogs, physical location):

_____

_____

_____

_____

Explanation/Justification of my wishes for my online presence once I have passed away:

_____

_____

_____

_____

_____

I have designated _____ (Name of Designee) as my Designated Digital Remains Steward to act as the person to carry out my wishes for my Digital Remains.

Date: _____   Signature:

_____

ACKNOWLEDGMENTS

Any attempt to portray how much help, support, and time is given by those around you while you're writing a book would be understated, to say the least. So many people have shown support and interest in this project. Together we have learned what it takes to usher a book from concept to publication, and I am grateful to have had you all by my side throughout this journey.

I would like to start by thanking my lovely wife, JoHannah, who endured a cross-country move, the launch of a new company, quarantining during a pandemic, and my adventure in publishing, all within our first year of marriage. *(The label "rock star" does not begin to describe how amazing she is.)* I would like to thank the various family members in the funeral industry who have shown both support and begrudging admiration for my pursuit to always be moving toward something.

Thank you to all my family: William Connor Harrington; Jeff Harrington; Pam Blankenship; Imogene Blankenship; Bill Blankenship, my grandfather who passed away during the writing of this book; John H. Harrington; Connie Harrington, my grandmother who had a great love of cobalt glass and is gone but not forgotten; Mary Ann Worthington, who brought a welcome light; Brad and Carrie Harrington; Stella Harrington; Lake Harrington; Sadie Harrington; Biff Blankenship; Biff and Toni Blankenship; Molly Blankenship; William Blankenship; Nikki and Josh Kirschner; Lyric Kirschner; Aisley Kirschner; Al and Christi Torkelson; Andy Torkelson and Ari Bertman; Avi Torkelson; and Clark and Linda Beier. Also, thanks to my close friends: Danny Thompson, who has been a constant supporter for too many years to count, and Rae Sedgwick and Andy Frazier, who offered needed breaks over coffee and spoke of past writing. Thank you to the communities that have been like a family to me: the East Village of Georgetown in Washington DC, Bonner Springs, KS, and Palo Alto, CA.

A special thanks to the professors who stood out in this unique field of study: Wiley Wright, Rick Sprick, Dr. Terry Martin, and Dr. Flavius Lilly. Thank you to all those who have shared your stories with me—which brought me to this point—in class discussions in the Thanatology Program, guest lectures, group sessions, hospice work, volunteer projects, counseling sessions, and in passing. Your stories have helped me form a depth of knowledge that could not be achieved in any other setting. Thank you.

Thank you to all of those both in front and behind the scenes at the Creator Institute, namely Eric Koester, who is motivation in a bottle, and his lead assistant Lyn Solares, who did so much behind the scenes.

Thank you to all those at New Degree Press. Brian Bies and his colleagues run an amazingly efficient team and were hands-on or hands-off when needed, a truly rare gift. Thanks to Publishing Coordinator Jamie Tibasco in contracting and promotions. Thank you also to my editors at New Degree Press: Head of Editing Leila Summers, who did more than I can imagine; Developmental Editor Michael Bailey, who encouraged and pulled ideas out of me I did not know I had; Acquiring Editor Lisa Patterson, you taught me so much; Marketing & Revisions Editor P. Richelle White, who guided me through publisher goals for personal pre-sales, made an amazing round of edits, and has a gift for cover inspiration; Head of Copy Editing Amanda Brown; and Copy Editor Extraordinaire Caitlin Panarella, who has a gift and turned this book into something beyond my hopes. Also special thanks to Cover Designer Aleksandra Dabic, Senior Layout Designer Vladimir Dudas, and Art Director Gjorgji Pejkovski.

Thank you to all those who shared personal stories and experiences with me, both in person and from afar. Know that your stories have made an impact on me and will make an impact on the many others who read them.

Thank you to all of those who showed their support during the presale of *Digital Remains*: **Robin Roberts, Pam Blankenship, Janelle Margolis, Daniel Thompson, David Cannady, Andrew Torkelson, Marjorie Bertman, Elaine Wright, Corbin Philip Burright, JoHannah Harrington, Christi and Al Torkelson, Mary Thompson, Andy and Catherine Frazier, Clark and Linda Beier, Larry Clark, Eric Koester, Stephanie Goraczkowski, Meridith Pumphrey,**

Emory James, James Hills, Keith Midberry, Margaret Hoversten, Barbara Helling, Elizabeth Doepke, Gretchen Viney, Jason Beier, Jeff Harrington, Conner Guyer, JoAnn Weinkauf, Robert A. Wachendorf, Ryan Muise, Jean and Tim Ney, William R. Downing, Susan Balzer, Michelle Frank, Rebecca McDermeit, Eric Waldon, Jack Shteamer, Larry Freidig, Margaret Dunn, Robin Ney, Don and Vicki Wheeler, Susan O'Meara Hernes, John Harrington, Mary Ann Worthington, Lori Holloway, Amit Puri, P. Richelle White, Lisa Linsenmeier, David Susens, Brent Wine, and C. Khari Knight. You inspired so much hope in me to pull this project to the finish line. Without patrons like you, I would not have been able to make this dream come true.

APPENDIX

INTRODUCTION

Center for Disease Control and Prevention. "Death and Mortality."
National Center for Health Statistics. Accessed on May 5, 2020.
https://www.cdc.gov/nchs/fastats/deaths.htm.

CHAPTER ONE

DIGGING DEEPER THAN SIX FEET UNDER

Fernando Gordillo, Lilia Mestas, José M. Arana, Miguel Ángel
Pérez, and Eduardo Alejandro Escotto. "The Effect of Mortality
Salience and Type of Life on Personality Evaluation." *Europe's
journal of psychology*, 13(2), 286–299. https://www.ncbi.nlm.nih.
gov/pmc/articles/PMC5450985/.

FORA.tv. "Designing the 'Six Feet Under' Title Sequence—Danny
Yount." January 15, 2010. Video, 4:42. https://www.youtube.
com/watch?v=X9iv5vnoZBo.

J. Greenberg, T. Pyszczynski, and S. Solomon. "The causes and consequences of the need for self-esteem: A terror management theory." In R. F. Baumeister (Ed.), *Public self and private self,* 189-212.

T. Pyszczynski, J. Greenberg, S. Solomon. "A dual-process model of defense against conscious and unconscious death-related thoughts: an extension of terror management theory." Psychological Review vol. 106,4 (1999): 835-45. doi:10.1037/0033-295x.106.4.835.

CHAPTER TWO
DEATH AND SOCIAL MEDIA

Gilbert, Ben. "It's been over 12 years since the iPhone debuted—look how primitive the first one seems today." *Business Insider,* July 22 2019. https://www.businessinsider.com/first-phone-anniversary-2016-12.

History.com Editors. "Facebook Launches." *A&E Television Networks,* October 24, 2019. https://www.history.com/this-day-in-history/facebook-launches-mark-zuckerberg.

Molina, Brett. "When is the right age to buy your child a smartphone?" *USA Today,* August 27, 2017. https://www.usatoday.com/story/tech/talkingtech/2017/08/24/when-right-age-buy-your-child-smartphone-wait-until-8-th/593195001/.

Phillips, Sarah. "A brief history of Facebook." *The Guardian,* July 25, 2007. https://www.theguardian.com/technology/2007/jul/25/media.newmedia.

CHAPTER THREE

FINDING THE WORDS

Gunning, Benjamin. "Words of Support." Instagram, January 21, 2020. Accessed January 22, 2020. https://www.instagram.com/p/B7mFiDeHoHI/.

CHAPTER FOUR

DIGITAL REMAINS

Facebook. "Memorialized Accounts" Help Center. Accessed May 28, 2020. https://www.facebook.com/help/1506822589577997.

Lexico. s.v. "QR code (n.)." Accessed May 28, 2020. https://www.lexico.com/definition/qr_code.

Ohman, Carl and Luciano Floridi. (2018). "An ethical framework for the digital afterlife industry." Nature Human Behaviour. 10.1038/s41562-018-0335-2.

URNING THE ANSWER:

WILL THE WORLD RUN OUT OF SPACE TO BURY THE DEAD?

Allain, Rhett. "How Much Dirt from This Diamond Mine?" *Wired.* January 22, 2013. https://www.wired.com/2013/01/how-much-dirt-from-this-diamond-mine/.

"AT&T Stadium." Twitter. Posted January 27, 2017. https://twitter.com/ATTStadium/status/825010836078997504.

Cremation Association of North America. "Industry Statistical Information." Accessed May 29, 2020. https://www.cremation-association.org/page/IndustryStatistics.

International Swimming Federation (FINA). "FINA Facilities Rules." Swimming Pools. Accessed April 28, 2020. https://www.fina.org/sites/default/files/finafacilities_rules.pdf.

United States Census. "State Area Measurements and Internal Point Coordinates." References Files. Accessed May 29, 2020. https://www.census.gov/geographies/reference-files/2010/geo/state-area.html.

United States Census. "U.S. and World Population Clock." U.S. Population. Accessed May 29, 2020. https://www.census.gov/popclock/.

United States Navy. "Facts File." AIRCRAFT CARRIERS - CVN. Accessed May 29, 2020. https://www.navy.mil/navydata/fact_display.asp?cid=4200&tid=200&ct=4.

University of Kansas. "Land Area and Population Density in Kansas, by County." Institute for Policy and Social Research. Accessed May 29, 2020. http://www.ipsr.ku.edu/ksdata/ksah/population/2pop23.pdf.

CHAPTER FIVE
THE PRINTED OBITUARY

Morton, John (October–November 2007). "Buffeted: Newspapers Are Paying the Price for Shortsighted Thinking." *American Journalism Review*. Archived from the original on 2008-10-10. Retrieved 2020-02-10.

Seamans, Robert and Feng Zhu (February 2014). "Responses to Entry in Multi-Sided Markets: The Impact of Craigslist on Local Newspapers" (PDF). *Management Science*. 60 (2): 476–493. Accessed May 29, 2020. CiteSeerX 10.1.1.306.9200. doi:10.1287/mnsc.2013.1785.

"Talk to the Newsroom: Obituaries Editor Bill McDonald." The New York Times. September 25, 2006. https://www.nytimes.com/2006/09/25/business/media/25asktheeditors.html.

CHAPTER SIX
LEARNING FROM THE END

Narayan, Lux. "Lux Narayan's debut set at the Comedy Cellar." Posted February 20, 2017. Video, 7:55. https://www.youtube.com/watch?v=nMrwt_ZaDq4.

Narayan, Lux. "What I Learned From 2,000 Obituaries." Filmed January 2017 at TEDNYC. Video, 6:00.

https://www.ted.com/talks/lux_narayan_what_i_learned_from_2_000_obituaries?language=en.

CHAPTER SEVEN
MODERN NOTIFICATIONS

IDC Research. "Always Connected." An IDC Research Report. Accessed May 29, 2020. https://www.nu.nl/files/IDC-Facebook%20Always%20Connected%20(1).pdf.

CHAPTER EIGHT

THE REACH OF SOCIAL MEDIA

Christakis, Nicholas. "The hidden influence of social networks." Filmed February 2010. Video, 28:07. https://www.ted.com/talks/nicholas_christakis_the_hidden_influence_of_social_networks/transcript

Elwert Christakis, Felix Christakis, and Nicholas Christakis. (2008). "The Effect of Widowhood on Mortality by the Causes of Death of Both Spouses." *American Journal of Public Health,* 98(11), 2092–2098.

URNING THE ANSWER:

ASHES, WHAT ARE THEY REALLY?

Dyer, Mary H. "Planting in Cremation Ashes – Are Cremation Ashes Good for Plants." Gardening Know-How. Accessed May 29, 2020. https://www.gardeningknowhow.com/garden-how-to/info/cremation-ashes-and-plants.htm

CHAPTER NINE

FROM VISIBLE TO USABLE

Hartsdale Pet Cemetery. "Our History." Accessed May 29, 2020. https://www.hartsdalepetcrematory.com/about-us/our-history/.

Kaathy. "Home Page." Accessed June 1, 2020. https://www.kaathy.com/.

Slovanian Australian Chamber of Commerce. "World's First Digital Tombstone – From Maribor Slovenia!" Published Jun 9,

2017. https://www.slovenianaustralianchamber.com.au/digital-tombstones-from-slovenia/.

The Church of Jesus Christ of the Latter-Day Saints. "Cremation is a custom in various parts of the world. Do Latter-day Saints practice it?" Accessed May 29, 2020. https://www.churchofjesuschrist.org/study/ensign/1991/08/i-have-a-question/do-latter-day-saints-practice-cremation?lang=eng.

CHAPTER TEN
THE FUTURE IS OPTIONS

Aquamation. "Our Process." Accessed on May 29, 2020. https://aquamationinfo.com/process/.

Better Place Forests. "Home Page." Accessed May 29, 2020. https://www.betterplaceforests.com/.

Capsula Mundi. "Capsula Mundi. Life never stops." Accessed May 29, 2020. https://www.capsulamundi.it/en/.

Celestis. "Space Memorial Destinations." Accessed June 1, 2020. https://pages.celestis.com/guide/?gclid=EAIaIQobChM-ItOTczK-v6QIVrx6tBhoYew8yEAAYASAAEgIOj_D_BwE.

Cilento, Karen. "Columbarium at Sea / Tin-Shun But." *ArchDaily*. Accessed May 12, 2020. <https://www.archdaily.com/62362/columbarium-at-sea-tin-shun-but/> ISSN 0719-8884

Columbia GSPP. "Death Lab." Accessed June 1, 2020. https://www.arch.columbia.edu/research/labs/3-death-lab.

Death Cafe. "What is Death Cafe." Accessed June 1, 2020. https:// deathcafe.com/what/.

DeathPositiveDC. "About Death Positive DC." Accessed on May 12, 2020. https://www.deathpositivedc.com/about_us.

Death Over Dinner. "Let's Have Dinner and Talk About Death." Accessed May 12, 2020. https://deathoverdinner.org/.

Eterneva. "One-of-a-kind, just like them." Accessed May 29, 2020. https://eterneva.com/loved-ones.

Federal Trade Commission. "The FTC Funeral Rule." Accessed June 1, 2020. https://www.consumer.ftc.gov/articles/0300-ftc-funeral-rule.

Grundhauser, Eric. "Eugene Shoemaker Is Still the Only Man Buried on the Moon." *Atlas Obscura*. Published October 22, 2018. https://www.atlasobscura.com/articles/eugene-shoemaker-buried-moon-celestis-nasa.

Holson, Laura. "As Funeral Crowdfunding Grows, So Do the Risks." *New York Times*, June 5, 2018. https://www.nytimes.com/2018/06/05/business/funerals-crowdsourcing-crowdfunding-scams.html.

Informed Final Choices. "Crestone End-of-Life Project." Accessed May 29, 2020. http://informedfinalchoices.org/crestone/.

Memory Forests. "Our Story." Accessed June 1, 2020. https://memoryforest.org/.

Scott, Pam. "A Word from the Executive Director." *KFDA Journal* *80*, no.8 (September/October 2019): 4.

Song, Shiyu. "Architecture of Afterlife: Future Cemetery in Metropolis." (Doctoral Thesis, the University of Hawai'i at Manoa, 2017). file:///Users/hannah/Downloads/Song_Shiyu_ Spring%202017%20(1).pdf.

Reimagine. "What We Do." Accessed May 12, 2020. https://lets-reimagine.org/.

CHAPTER ELEVEN
VIRTUAL FUNERALS
Porter, Catherine. "A New Way To Mourn." April 24, 2020 in The Daily, podcast, 46:35. https://www.nytimes.com/2020/04/24/ podcasts/the-daily/coronavirus-deaths-grief.html?.

CHAPTER TWELVE
HOW DID WE GET HERE?
Cremation Association of North America (CANA). "Industry Statistical Information." Accessed June 1, 2020. https://www. cremationassociation.org/page/IndustryStatistics.

National Museum of Civil War Medicine. "Embalming and the Civil War." Posted on February 20, 2016. http://www.civil-warmed.org/embalming1/.

Pettitt, Paul. "Hominin evolutionary thanatology from the mortuary to funerary realm: the palaeoanthropological bridge between chemistry and culture." *Philosophical Transactions of the Royal Society B, Biological Sciences* 373, no.1754 (July 2018). https://royalsocietypublishing.org/doi/full/10.1098/rstb.2018.0212#d3e799.

Pillsbury, Katherine H. "*Duxbury, A Guide.*" Duxbury: Duxbury Rural and Historical Society (1999), 34.

URNING THE ANSWER:
THE PINE BOX PARADOX

CHAPTER THIRTEEN
DEATHITECTURE

Ariès, Philippe. *The Hour of Our Death: The Classic History of Western Attitudes Toward Death Over the Last One Thousand Years.* Vintage; 2 edition (July 22, 2008).

Columbia GSPP. "Death Lab." Accessed June 1, 2020. https://www.arch.columbia.edu/research/labs/3-death-lab.

Non Architecture Competitions. "Light After Life." Accessed June 1, 2020. https://www.nonarchitecture.eu/portfolio/light-after-life/.

CHAPTER FOURTEEN
THE LEGACY OF A LIKENESS

Dodson, Aaron. "The strange legacy of Tupac's 'hologram' lives on five years after its historic Coachella debut." *The Undefeated.* April 14, 2017. https://theundefeated.com/features/the-strange-legacy-of-tupacs-hologram-after-coachella/.

Ostrow, Adam. "After Your Final Status Update." Filmed July 2011 at TEDGlobal 2011. Video, 5:14. https://www.ted.com/talks/adam_ostrow_after_your_final_status_update/transcript?language=en.

Robinson, Cori. "Death and The Holograms: Celebrities Continue To Generate Revenue And Problems After Death." *Above The Law.* November 6, 2018. https://abovethelaw.com/2018/11/death-and-the-holograms-celebrities-continue-to-generate-revenue-and-problems-after-death/.

THE SOCIAL MEDIA CLEAN-UP GUIDE

Das, Mesheeka. "TikTok again took a young man's life, fell into the river but still no clue was found." *News Track Live.* September 30, 2019. https://english.newstracklive.com/news/tik-tok-video-4-friends-jump-off-bridge-into-river-death-crime-news-sc103-nu-1039657-1.html.

Hussaini, Syed Umarullah. "Sialkot Boy Loses Life Taping Tik Tok Video." *BOL News.* December 29, 2019. https://www.bolnews.com/pakistan/2019/12/sialkot-boy-loses-life-taping-tik-tok-video/.

Instagram. "How do I report a deceased person's account on Instagram?" Help Center. Privacy and Safety Center. Accessed June 1, 2020. https://help.instagram.com/264154560391256.

LinkedIn. "Request removal of a deceased member's LinkedIn profile." Contact Us. Accessed June 1, 2020. https://www.linkedin.com/help/linkedin/ask/TS-RDMLP?lang=en.

Pinterest. "Privacy Policy." Accessed June 1, 2020. https://policy.pinterest.com/en/privacy-policy.

Snapchat. "Snapchat Support." Contact Us. Accessed June 1, 2020. https://support.snapchat.com/en-US/i-need-help?start=5640758388326400.

Statista. "Most popular social networks worldwide as of April 2020, ranked by number of active users." Social Media and User-Generated Content. Accessed June 1, 2020. https://www.statista.com/statistics/272014/global-social-networks-ranked-by-number-of-users/.

TikTok. "Contact." Accessed June 1, 2020. https://www.tiktok.com/about?lang=en.

Twitter. "How to contact Twitter about a deceased family member's account." Rules and Policies. Accessed on May 28, 2020. https://help.twitter.com/en/rules-and-policies/contact-twitter-about-a-deceased-family-members-account.